Parent and Child Fostering

Paul Adams and Elaine Dibben

BAAF

ADOPTION
& FOSTERING

Published by
British Association for Adoption & Fostering
(BAAF)
Saffron House
6-10 Kirby Street
London EC1N 8TS
www.baaf.org.uk

Charity registration 275689 (England and Wales) and SC039337 (Scotland)
© BAAF, 2011

British Library Cataloguing in Publication Data
A catalogue record for this book is available from the British Library

ISBN 978 1 907585 30 2

Project management by Shaila Shah, BAAF
Designed and typeset by Helen Joubert Design
Printed in Great Britain by the Lavenham Press

BAAF is the leading UK-wide membership organisation for all those
concerned with adoption, fostering and child care issues.

Contents

Acknowledgements

The content of this guide was developed at two focus days held in Leeds and London in November 2010 and we would like to acknowledge the contribution of all the fostering services that were represented at those days and are named below.

We are grateful to those attendees who subsequently contributed to this Good Practice Guide by sending in case examples and proformas to be included in the guide. These have assisted us in illustrating practice and offering readers the opportunity to benefit from the work that has already been developed in this area.

We would particularly like to thank Sharon Donnelly, Suzanne Lyus, Kim Taylor, Peter Turner and Janice Rutherford for reading a draft version and providing valuable feedback and Rachel Taylor from the Fostering Policy team at the Department for Education, who has assisted us in providing clarity in the areas where parent and child arrangements fall outside of fostering regulations.

Finally, we would like to thank John Simmonds for his wisdom, guidance and encouragement; Shaila Shah and her team for helping us achieve the final product; and most significantly, Cate Walker, whose role in co-ordinating materials, chasing up contributors and providing high quality administration has been central to the production of this guide.

This guide has kindly been supported by the following funders:

Garfield Weston Foundation
Esmée Fairbairn Foundation

Fostering providers and BAAF staff represented at the Parent and Child Focus Days

John Beasty – ISP Childcare Rainham

Lisa Beaton – West Sussex County Council

Tonie Bull – Focused Fostering

Alexandra Conroy Harris – Legal Consultant, BAAF

Vicky Davidson-Boyd – Team Fostering and North East Fostering Network Forum

Gwyn Davies – Foster carer, Brighton and Hove Council

Sharon Donnelly – Brighton and Hove Council

Nick Dunster – Regional Director, BAAF

Wendy Edgell – Foster Care Associates Eastern Region

Jayne Ford – Fostering Outcomes

Margaret Gardiner – Care UK (now Care Tech Foster Care)

Kate Hamilton-Harris – Kasper Fostering

Joanna Hide – Southampton Council

Joy Jeffries – East Sussex County Council
Liz Khan – London Borough of Islington
Kim Leighton – Team Fostering
Suzanne Lyus – Somerset County Council
Keith Miller – Regional Trainer/Consultant, BAAF
Jo Oliver – Chrysalis Care
Ceri Orton – Leeds Social Care
Beverley Peat – Greater London Fostering
Roana Roach –Trainer/Consultant, BAAF
Claire Rogers – North Lincolnshire Council
Fiona Rose – Families for Children
Janice Rutherford –The Adolescent and Children's Trust (TACT)
Joanne Salmon – Fostering People
Brenda Smith – Foster carer, SWIIS Foster Care
Kim Taylor – Pathway Care
Angela Tobin – Foster Care Co-operative
Peter Turner – Fostering People Too
Karen Van Bosch – Outlook Fostering

Notes about the authors

Paul Adams qualified as a social worker in 1993, having been inspired by working as a foster carer in the US. He has worked predominantly in local authority children's services, managing child care and fostering teams.

Paul joined BAAF as a Fostering Development Consultant in 2010. He chairs both fostering and adoption panels, sits on GSCC registration and conduct committees, and provides consultancy and training. He has published research on parent and child fostering.

He lives in North Wales with his partner Sarah, and rescue dogs Simba and Bluebell.

Elaine Dibben started her social work career in residential social work and qualified in 1988. She has over 20 years' experience of working in fostering and adoption in local authority and voluntary agency settings and now chairs both fostering and adoption panels.

She joined BAAF in 2004 to become manager of the Independent Review Mechanism which she set up and ran until 2009 when she moved to take on a wider role in BAAF as a trainer/consultant. She is currently a Fostering and Adoption Development Consultant for BAAF and published her first book with BAAF in 2010, *Undertaking an Adoption Assessment: A guide to collecting and analysing information for the Prospective Adopter's Report (formerly Form F) England.*

Elaine lives in Oxfordshire with her husband, Steve, and their two cats Mabel and Cleo.

Introduction

Parent and child arrangements with foster carers are a rapidly growing phenomenon, in England and Wales particularly, and to a lesser extent in Northern Ireland. In Scotland, this type of parent and child arrangement is not used very much.[1] While accurate national data about its use are not available, the anecdotal evidence from local authority fostering services and independent fostering services suggests that its use is widespread. Some local authorities have established whole teams to deal with this expanding area of work, and some independent services in England suggest that these cases constitute up to 10 per cent of their total referrals.

Historically, when parents – usually mothers – needed to be assessed with their babies or children, this was undertaken within a residential care setting. The advantage of this as a placement choice was that it was a safe setting for both mother and baby with the availability of expertise in assessment and support in care, parenting and other significant issues such as mental health. Although there have always been examples of parents being fostered with their children, these have tended to be ad hoc arrangements designed to allow teenage parents, often themselves looked after, to remain with their baby. The emphasis in these arrangements has largely been on supporting rather than formally assessing the quality of parenting.

In recent years, however, in England and Wales particularly, there have been two key drivers contributing to a significant expansion in parent and child fostering.

Firstly, it is evident that even where there are significant child protection concerns, courts are increasingly reluctant to separate parents from their babies. Justice Munby[2] described the separation of a parent and child as a 'draconian and extremely harsh measure which demands extraordinarily compelling justification'. This is an approach that has been supported by a number of judgements made by the European Court of Human Rights (ECHR; Prior, 2003, p. 184), and it is further suggested that CAFCASS guardians are now less inclined to agree plans for assessment that require parents to be living apart from their children.

---

1   There is little court involvement in arrangements for day-to-day care or assessments, as the hearing system is the forum where a lot of these matters are dealt with. However, the extensive practice information in this guide should still be helpful to practitioners in Scotland.

2   *Re M* (Care Proceedings: Judicial Review) [2003] EWHC 850 (Admin), [2003] 2 FLR 171).

The judgement in *Re M* has also had an impact on attitudes to contact where parents and babies are living apart from each other. Justice Munby cited the ECHR as reason for requiring high levels of daily contact between a baby and mother, enough to allow her to breastfeed the child (Humphreys and Kiraly, 2011; Schofield and Simmonds, 2011). An obvious solution to this dilemma is to arrange for the parent and child to be placed together, either in a residential setting or in fostering, and it would appear that this is what has increasingly been happening.

The second driver has been financial, resulting from changes to legal aid funding in England and Wales in October 2007, which has meant that no costs relating to a residential assessment of a child could be charged to the Legal Services Commission (England), leaving the local authority responsible for these costs. Taylor (2008) suggests that this resulted in a reduction of residential placements and an increase in fostering placements, because the latter are considerably cheaper.

In response to this increased demand for parent and child fostering, local authorities and independent fostering agencies in England and Wales began to develop their services to meet this need, and this has resulted in pockets of expertise being developed in different places and slightly different local contexts. Where previously this type of fostering tended to be offered to children who became mothers while in the care system, the new demand was for placements of adults with their children, usually in the context of care proceedings.

While some fostering services have developed their provision for parent and child arrangements, learning from their experience as they go, others have sought advice and guidance about how best to deliver parent and child fostering, and looked to identify best practice. There has been recognition that there are considerable challenges in what is a very specialist area of work. Early indications suggest that parent and child fostering arrangements can be hugely successful, whether the child remains with their birth parent or whether the outcome is separation, but providing a good quality parent and child fostering resource is not easy.

It is in this context that BAAF identified the need to produce practice guidance. In late 2010 meetings were arranged for practitioners from local authority and independent fostering services in England and Wales who were actively involved in developing and providing parent and child arrangements to explore the issues. On some aspects there was agreed best practice, in others there were as many questions as answers, and this guide has emerged from discussions at those groups and elsewhere.

We are very grateful to everyone who participated in those events, and who subsequently shared materials and case examples that are included in or have informed the content of this practice guide.

NOTE ON TERMINOLOGY

Historically, social workers and others have tended to talk about "mother and baby" fostering and many practitioners continue to use this term. We have preferred "parent and child" in recognition of the fact that increasing numbers of fathers are involved, and on occasions whole families, and also to recognise that not all of the children are babies. We are mindful of arguments that the child should be named first as in "child and parent", but have kept with the more recognised wording that emphasises the unique aspect of this arrangement – the involvement of a parent in a foster home.

Less easy is the question of whether we talk about parent and child "placements" or parent and child "arrangements". The Fostering Services (England) Regulations 2011 introduced a definition of parent and child arrangements as 'arrangements made by a local authority for a parent and their child to live with a foster parent, whether or not the parent or the child is placed with the foster parent'. In other words, the new term "parent and child arrangement" was introduced in recognition that these arrangements might be placements (a term with a specific legal meaning in England [3]), or they might not.

After much consideration we have decided to use this new term in the practice guidance although it is worth acknowledging that this is not without difficulties. Firstly, it is an England-specific term, and may not be recognised in other countries within the UK. For this we apologise, but have found ourselves caught between wanting to make this guidance relevant to all countries in the UK, and at the same time not wanting to use terminology that is technically incorrect in England, and that fails to convey the legal basis under which parents and children are living with people who are approved as foster carers.

The second difficulty is that "arrangements" is not a term being used by practitioners, even in England, and in the short term may cause some confusion even though it is now enshrined in legislation. In this guidance many of the appendices and good practice examples will contain the terminology of "placements", reflecting the fact that these have been in place pre-April 2011. In reality, it will take some time for practitioners to adjust to this new term and will mean that recognised terms like "pre-placement" and "post- placement" are replaced with "pre-arrangement" and "post-arrangement". We will also talk about "assessment arrangements", "support arrangements" and "holding arrangements",

---

3   "Placement" is defined in the Care Planning, Placement and Case Review (England) Regulations 2010 as '(i) arrangements made by the responsible authority for C to live with P in accordance with section 22C(2), where C is in the care of the responsible authority, or (ii) arrangements made by the responsible authority to provide for C's accommodation and maintenance by any means specified in section 22C(6).'

rather than using these terms to define different "placements". These phrases will likely feel unfamiliar and uncomfortable for some time.

We have used the definitions set out in the England Regulations 2011 when describing the different fostering services, so the generic term "fostering services" is used to cover both local authority fostering services and independent fostering agencies. We have also used the term "independent fostering agencies" as defined in 4(4) of the Care Standards Act 2000 rather than "fostering service providers" which is defined as relating to the registered person in a fostering agency in the England Regulations 2011.

1

The legal context of parent and child arrangements

In the legislation governing fostering in the four countries, there has been no recognition of foster carers as providers of parent and child arrangements. However, as practice has developed, local authorities, Health and Social Care Trusts in Northern Ireland,[4] and independent fostering services have had to consider carefully how current legislation applies to parent and child fostering.

ENGLAND

The fostering statutory framework provides for approval and assessment of foster carers to act as "local authority foster parents" for looked after children. The key primary legislation (the Children Act 1989 and the Care Standards Act 2000) did not envisage foster carers undertaking parent and child assessment activity as at that time such work was undertaken in residential family centres. Therefore, the scope of the fostering statutory framework covers fostering of looked after children and not other activity which may be undertaken in the foster home such as parenting assessment or support in the foster home to non-looked after children. As practice has developed, local authorities and fostering services have had to consider carefully how current legislation applies to the various individual situations within parent and child fostering.

Parent and child fostering arrangements must, depending on the legal status of parent and child, comply with the Care Planning, Placement and Case Review (England) Regulations 2010 (the 2010 Regulations), and The Fostering Services (England) Regulations 2011 (the 2011 Regulations). Fostering services will also need to be aware of the Statutory Guidance (Volume 4: *Fostering Services*) updated in 2011, that specifically addresses the issue of parent and child fostering in paragraphs 2.14–2.16 and in Annex B (Volume 4: *Fostering Services*).

---

4   Where local authorities are referenced in the remainder of this guide, this reference will include Health and Social Care Trusts in Northern Ireland where relevant.

Annex B (set out in full in Appendix 1) sets out the legal status in different parent and child scenarios, and has brought clarity to three key issues that had previously been challenging fostering services.

- A foster carer's household is not an establishment, and so cannot be regarded as a residential family centre, meaning that the Residential Family Centre Regulations 2002 do not apply to a fostering household.

- A person who is living with a foster carer as part of a parent and child arrangement is a member of the foster carer's household for the purposes of the regulations. What this means is that a parent of a child, who may be an adult, is a part of the fostering household, with all that this implies in terms of the suitability of the household to foster. The Statutory Guidance (Annex B, 12) makes clear that there is no requirement for a CRB check to be completed prior to another person joining the household, but does require that 'the fostering service's safeguarding policy must include a statement of measures to be taken to safeguard children placed with foster carers before any arrangements are made for a parent and child to join the household'. This raises questions about whether and, if so, how other types of fostering can safely take place alongside such parent and child fostering arrangements, and this is discussed in greater depth elsewhere in this practice guidance.

- It is important to note that where a parent has committed a specified offence they cannot be considered for a parent and child arrangement under fostering regulations, because they would be deemed a member of that fostering household.

It is not always straightforward to understand how to apply the relevant legislation to parent and child arrangements. It will depend on the legal status of the child and the parent, as well as the local authority's views on the specific factors in each case. The Statutory Guidance (2.14) states that:

> when arrangements are made for a parent and child to live together with foster carers...the responsible authority must take particular care to clarify the nature of the arrangement...In whichever circumstance, it will be necessary to clarify the respective roles of the foster carer and the parent in relation to the child.

There are four basic legal scenarios that apply to parent and child fostering, with different implications depending on the regulations that apply.

1) Where the parent is under 18 and is looked after by the local authority and the child is looked after by the local authority, each will be subject to all the requirements of the 2010 Care Planning and 2011 Fostering Regulations. In this scenario, the regulations in relation to placement with parents (2010, 15–20) will not apply.

2) Where the parent is under 18 and is looked after by the local authority it may be that their looked after child is placed with them under regulations in relation to placement with parents (2010, 15–20). Under this scenario the requirements of the 2010 Care Planning Regulations will apply to both parent and child, but the 2011 Fostering Regulations will apply only to the parent.

3) Where a parent is under 18 but is not looked after, or over 18, but their child is looked after by the local authority, only the child will be subject to all the requirements of the 2010 Care Planning and 2011 Fostering Regulations. In this scenario, regulations in relation to placement with parents (2010, 15–20) will not apply, and the parent will be considered as part of the fostering household.

4) Where a parent is under 18 but is not looked after, or over 18, and the local authority takes the view that the child is being cared for by their parent and does not need to be looked after, then both may reside in what would normally be a foster home, but neither the 2010 Care Planning nor the 2011 Fostering Regulations will apply to either the child or parent.

It is clear from the above scenarios that local authority and independent fostering services will need to carefully consider the benefits or risks associated with each of these in relation to the specific needs in individual cases.

In circumstances where neither the 2010 nor the 2011 Regulations apply, the local authority will need to be particularly careful to ensure that the arrangements are safe and appropriate, and Statutory Guidance (2.14) reminds us that 'the fostering service should be mindful of the additional responsibilities of the foster carer, any additional skills, training and support the carer may require, and any additional insurance considerations'. It will also be necessary to take account of the needs of any foster child living in the household.

If a local authority or fostering service is considering making arrangements that do not fall under one or both of the 2010 or 2011 Regulations, they will need to think carefully about whether the arrangements are sufficiently structured, or whether another legal arrangement might be better, and what action might be necessary to ensure that everyone is clear about their roles and responsibilities. Specifically, the local authority might want to consider whether another arrangement might be more appropriate, such as accommodating either parent or child or both, or considering whether grounds are met for applying for a care order.

They also need to ensure that their insurance covers arrangements that do not fall within current legislation.

WALES

At the time of this publication, the Welsh regulatory framework remains unrevised and therefore the fostering aspects of a parent and child arrangement are covered by the Fostering Services (Wales) Regulations 2003, the Placement of Children (Wales) Regulations 2007, the Review of Children Cases (Wales) Regulations 2007, and the Placement of Children with Parents Regulations 1991. It is anticipated that the Welsh Assembly Government will consult on the new regulations during the summer of 2011, and parent and child arrangements will likely be addressed within this.

The four legal scenarios, as set out in the legal context for England, are the same for Wales, with the relevant Welsh regulations applying. As it currently stands, there is a general consensus, although not clearly set out in legislation, that an arrangement which is compliant with the fostering regulations and placement with parent regulations is a lawful arrangement.

There has been some confusion in the past in Wales as to whether a parent and child arrangement falls within the definition of a residential family centre and is therefore subject to the Residential Family Centre (Wales) Regulations 2003. Although there is nothing in any of the regulations which indicates that such arrangements should be subject to this framework, it has been the intention of the Welsh Assembly Government to seek an amendment to the regulations and to add parent and child arrangements with foster carers to the list of exemptions set out in Regulation 3. This amendment has yet to be made but it is anticipated that the new regulations will clarify that such arrangements are exempt.

The Care and Social Services Inspectorate Wales produced guidance for inspectors in 2009, which sets out guidance for arrangements where the parent is considered to be in an adult placement or care home if personal care is being offered to the parent.

It also sets out good practice guidance in relation to the legal framework for the arrangement. In particular, where the parent is under 18, the authority should have undertaken an assessment of their needs to inform the decision on whether they should also be looked after and clarifies that:

> ...where both the parent and child are placed by the fostering service, there are two separate placements for the purposes of limits of foster children pursuant to Schedule 7 Children Act 1998 (the usual fostering limit).

The guidance confirms the need for foster carers to have the necessary skills to be able to care for both parent and child and provides a list of considerations for inspectors, which includes assessment, training, support and the need for policies and procedures.

The guidance also states that:

> CSSIW are of the view that it is not good practice for a foster carer to be providing an 'assessment' placement for more than one parent and child(ren) at a time. This is not supported by regulations but we should consider making a good practice recommendation where we find multiple parent and child placements with a carer, depending on the circumstances of the individual case.

In relation to the placement agreement the guidance states:

> The foster placement agreement for the child should make very clear the roles and responsibilities of the parent and foster carer in relation to the child. The placing authority must be explicit in this agreement about who is responsible for the child and what the expectations of the foster carer are especially in relation to reporting arrangements.

It further suggests that the agreement should make provision for a variation in those responsibilities as circumstances change.

NORTHERN IRELAND

There is no specific reference in Fostering Regulations or Placement with Parent Regulations that cover parent and child fostering arrangements in Northern Ireland.

The following regulations will need to be considered:

- The Arrangements for Placement of Children (General) Regulations (Northern Ireland) 1996
- The Foster Placement (Children) Regulations (Northern Ireland) 1996
- The Placement of Children with Parents etc Regulations (Northern Ireland) 1996

The definition of a residential family centre is in Article 2 of the Health and Personal Social Services (Quality, Improvement and Regulation) (Northern Ireland) Order 2003 and says:

> "residential family centre" means, subject to paragraph (8), any establishment at which:

> (a) accommodation is provided for children and their parents;

> (b) the parents' capacity to respond to the children's needs and to safeguard their welfare is monitored or assessed; and

(c) the parents are given such advice, guidance or counselling as is considered necessary;

and in this definition "parent", in relation to a child, includes any person who is looking after the child.

Standards for Residential Family Centres were announced at the end of March 2011 by the Health Minister and will be operant from 1 April 2011. There is no clarification on whether these apply to parent and child arrangements in foster homes.

SCOTLAND

As indicated in the introduction, this type of fostering placement is not used much in Scotland and there has been little service development. The children's hearing system is the main forum for processing assessments of looked after children and their families, particularly in short- to medium-term situations. Overall, the Scottish context does not lend itself to much need for or use of parent and child fostering placements.

Young people in Scotland acquire full civil capacity when they become 16. Parents can have parental responsibilities and rights even under the age of 16. In practice, relatively few young people continue to be looked after beyond 16, particularly through the hearing system.

Children and young people under 18 who are in foster care are "looked after", under s.17(6) of the Children (Scotland) Act 1995. The Looked After Children (Scotland) Regulations 2009 deal with arrangements for all looked after children, including those in foster placements; and they also deal with the assessment, approval and review of all public foster carers, whether by local authorities or registered fostering services. All fostering placements are covered by the 2009 Regulations.

Assessments of risk and of children's and parents' relationships, attachments, contact, etc, are carried out in a variety of settings, for example, children may be in foster care and separated from parents; children and parents may be placed together in residential assessment centres or other locations; or children may return or remain at home. Many children in the hearing system are looked after at home, so assessment work may be undertaken while children live with parent(s) and are simultaneously protected by their "home" supervision requirements.

If the child is looked after in foster care and the parent lives with the child but is not looked after, the 2009 Regulations apply to the placement. The foster carers must be approved under the 2009

Regulations. If a parent is looked after in foster care with the child, the placement is subject to the 2009 Regulations, like any other fostering placement. The carers must be approved under the 2009 Regulations. If both the parent and child are looked after, both placements are subject to the 2009 Regulations. The carers must be approved under the 2009 Regulations.

When a local authority makes plans for and recommendations about any looked after parent and/or child, it must do so in terms of its general duties in s.17 of the Children (Scotland) Act 1995, and its duties in the 2009 Regulations. These duties include safeguarding and promoting the looked after parent and/or child's welfare as its paramount concern, s.17(1)(a). It must also take account of the views of the looked after person and parents and other relatives. When a hearing or court makes decisions about any looked after parent and/or child, the overarching principles apply to them, including the welfare of the looked after person as their paramount consideration, in terms of s.16 of the 1995 Act.

Where the parent and child are both looked after, the local authority, hearing and court all need to balance their duties to both of them, when planning, recommending or making decisions. They need to be clear that there are two separate looked after people and that the two plans fit together. Where only the child is looked after, strictly speaking these duties only apply to plans, decisions, etc, for and about her or him. But there should also be consideration of the parent's position. Where only the parent is looked after, strictly speaking the duties only apply to plans, decisions, etc, for and about her or him. But there should also be consideration of the child's position.

It is also necessary that insurance arrangements for looked after children and young people, and for foster carers, cover situations where children and parents are placed together in foster placements.

2

Messages from research and serious case reviews

INTRODUCTION

Although there have been no large-scale research studies on parent and child arrangements, there have been a number of small studies using primarily qualitative approaches, and two relevant serious case reviews. The scale of the studies means some caution is needed in reaching any firm conclusions, but there are a number of common themes and much valuable information about what appears to make these arrangements work well, and what policy and practice is needed to support this.

THE DATA

The studies

There have been only two studies containing any sort of quantitative element, both of them undertaken within individual local authorities.

Martin and Davies (2007)

Martin and Davies (2007) looked at the quality and outcomes of 39 parent and baby arrangements made between January 2005 and August 2006 in West Sussex involving 34 children (some of whom had more than one arrangement). Information on each case was gathered from existing databases and questionnaires were completed by 79 per cent of the social workers involved in these cases.

About three-quarters of these parent and baby arrangements in the sample were provided by independent fostering services, with the remainder evenly split between residential units and "in-house" foster carers. The length of the arrangements varied from two days to over a year, and the parents were all mothers aged between 14–35 years, but most likely to be in their late teens. About 40 per cent of the mothers were known to have been looked after, or were being looked after at the point the arrangement started, and most were white British. The children were mainly babies aged between one and two months but included toddlers up to two years and ten months old, and the sample also included pregnant mothers.

Donnelly and Wright (2009)

Donnelly and Wright (2009) looked at the outcomes of 61 parent and baby assessment arrangements made in Brighton and Hove during 2004–2008. This used quantitative data already gathered, alongside interviews with carers, parents, social work and health staff.

The vast majority of the arrangements in the sample were parent and child fostering (51) with the other arrangements being in residential settings. Most arrangements were of mothers and their children but two involved a father and child. Ten of the parents were either currently or previously in care. The average length of the arrangement was six months, ranging from two weeks to nearly two years.

Other small-scale studies have tended to take a more qualitative approach, based primarily on interviews with foster carers and/or young mothers in parent and child arrangements.

Knight et al (2006)

Knight et al (2006) mention mother and baby fostering in the context of a much wider Department of Health-funded study on teenage pregnancy among young people who were either in care or leaving care. The study includes interviews with six young mothers in foster care, and with two foster carers. Although parent and child fostering was not the main focus of this study, it did reveal the growing use of foster carers to support young mothers in the care of their babies. Chase et al (2009) used this same data set in a different publication.

Greenaway (2010)

Greenaway (2010) interviewed five foster carers and one birth parent who were involved in parent and child fostering with the Somerset Family Assessment and Support Team, a specialist parent and child fostering scheme.

Adams and Bevan (2011)

Adams and Bevan (2011) interviewed eight mother and baby carers who fostered for three fostering services within the North West London Fostering Consortium. They had fostered 16 mothers and babies between them. The mothers were aged between 13–30 with the majority (about two-thirds) being under 18 and mostly themselves looked after. Information was also sought from the three local authority fostering services that participated in the study about their use of mother and baby arrangements and any policies and procedures that were used within their service.

The serious case reviews

The other important information comes from two serious case reviews involving parent and child arrangements.

Bromley Serious Case Review (2008)

Child B was subject to a child protection plan and had been living with his mother in a parent and child arrangement in a foster home. His mother took him from the foster home to stay at her mother's house, and three days later he died from sudden unexpected death in infancy after sleeping on the sofa with her. The serious case review sought to ascertain whether there had been sufficient assessments completed and whether Child B should also have been subject to legal proceedings.

Brent Serious Case Review (2009)

This case related to Child D who was placed with his mother in a foster home, where she had previously lived. There was another baby, Child F who was also placed with his mother in that foster home. Six weeks after his birth, Child D was admitted to hospital critically ill due to suspected salt poisoning, and it was later concluded during care proceedings that the overwhelming likelihood was that the mother of Child F was responsible for contaminating his feed. At the conclusion of the care proceedings, Child D was returned to the care of his mother.

EMERGING THEMES

Arising from this important but limited evidence, it is possible to identify a number of emerging themes. It is worth noting that in a number of these cases the researchers were unaware of each others' studies, but nevertheless came to similar conclusions.

1 Positive benefits of parent and child fostering

There is a consensus that parent and child fostering can offer a very effective way of supporting parents to care for their children. However, there is a need for more evidence that includes comparison groups and longer-term outcome data. Nevertheless, there is positive anecdotal evidence from both foster carers and mothers using the arrangements. Knight *et al* (2006) found that specialist mother and baby arrangements in a foster home appeared to be providing effective support to younger parents in care under the age of 16, and that such arrangements could potentially provide valuable support to older young parents. Adams and Bevan (2011) did not specifically ask about outcomes, but in the majority of cases foster carers were aware that the mothers had continued to care for their babies after leaving the foster home, and they talked about this making them feel that their efforts had been worthwhile.

The Brent SCR found that the parent and child arrangement they considered was able to provide much needed security and support to both of the young people and their babies and that the level of professional support offered enabled both mothers to demonstrate some good parenting skills when their babies were born.

The suggestion that parent and child fostering can work well is also indicated by the local authority studies. Donnelly and Wright (2009) note that of the 61 arrangements considered in the Brighton and Hove sample, just over half the children returned to the community with their parents. Although this does not in itself provide evidence that the parenting in these cases had improved, it is clear that professionals at least had been satisfied that any perceived risk had been reduced. Donnelly and Wright (2009) do identify the need for a longitudinal evaluation to consider the longer-term outcomes of these arrangements. In West Sussex (Martin and Davies, 2007) parenting skills were assessed before and after each arrangement and in 30 per cent of the cases they showed significant improvement and were rated as good at the end of the arrangement. The arrangements were seen to be of significant benefit in developing parenting skills in 43 per cent of cases.

It should also be noted that significant numbers of children in both of these local authority studies were unable to remain with birth parents, and permanence was progressed elsewhere. If parent and child fostering allowed for a fair, timely and effective assessment – although the data do not allow us to take a view on this either way – then this too could be deemed a positive outcome. In acknowledging the positive benefits of such placements, it must also be recognised (Donnelly and Wright, 2009; Adams and Bevan, 2011) that the work can also be challenging, both for the foster carers and also for the parents.

2 Roles, responsibilities and pre-arrangement planning

Another clearly defined theme is the importance of ensuring that the various roles and responsibilities of all parties are clearly established and understood, and good pre-arrangement planning is crucial in achieving this. A number of the studies make the point that clarity about roles and responsibilities is a key factor when things go well, and equally, lack of clarity is a factor when things go wrong (Adams and Bevan, 2011; Greenaway 2010). Foster carers themselves note the importance of clear written agreements, including clarity about contact with partner or family (Donnelly and Wright, 2009), with one foster carer (quoted in Adams and Bevan, 2011, p. 35) explaining the real practical benefits of this:

> I could say to her 'You go and look at your contract'...[it covered] what her role was and what mine was and when the father could visit...[and] when I'd look after the baby for her.

Knight *et al* (2006) also raise concerns over the lack of clarity about the responsibilities and roles of foster carers in relation to both the mother and baby in the arrangement; were they offering support or assessing the young parent? These issues are also important in relation to the expectations of the social workers involved. They suggest a need for national guidelines to support foster carers supporting young mothers and their children and for clarity around some of the day-to-day complexities of providing this specialist support.

In thinking about planning arrangements, it is important not to forget the practical issues such as finances and any agreed respite support for foster carers (Greenaway, 2010; Adams and Bevan, 2011).

Not surprisingly, a key issue in the Brent SCR was about the extent to which it was appropriate to have more than one parent and child living with the foster carer in the home at the same time. This issue is discussed elsewhere in this practice guidance. The SCR also highlighted that where a parent is looked after, the statutory reviews should maintain a clear focus on the individual's holistic needs with issues of parenting being appropriately and separately addressed. It also raised the importance of good communication between the respective social workers allocated to a looked after young mother and her child and this could be equally applied where there are two reviewing officers involved.

3 Relationship between foster carer and parent

The importance of the relationship between the foster carer and the parent is a theme raised in a number of studies, and the significance of this in terms of enabling positive outcomes. Greenaway (2010) notes that, where the parent made progress, this was reflected in the relationship between the carer and parent but where a lack of trust and communication developed between the parent and carer, this led to deterioration in the overall outcomes. Adams and Bevan (2011) make a similar point, concluding that a key factor in successful outcomes was whether the mother wanted to be in the foster home, and whether she "fitted in". Where this was the case, there was mutual warmth: parents felt able to accept advice and guidance, and carers felt a pride in the mother's achievements. Donnelly and Wright (2009) note that for some parents their experience in a parent and child arrangement is the first time they have received nurturing and warmth, something many of them had never seen in their birth families.

Where adult parents are placed this is not always easy, and in some cases parents are older than the foster carers, may have had previous children removed, and may feel disempowered and resentful to find themselves living with foster carers at that stage of their lives (Donnelly and Wright, 2009). It is suggested that if this cannot be addressed, then this might prove difficult for both parties.

It is suggested that arrangements worked better where birth parents have had the opportunity to meet with foster carers before the arrangement began, and with mothers who are themselves looked after, it is advantageous if they can move in before the baby is born (Donnelly and Wright, 2009; Greenaway, 2010; Adams and Bevan, 2011). Foster carers in the Donnelly and Wright (2009) study suggested that new mothers (moving in after giving birth) needed the first two weeks to settle into the home, often feeling particularly vulnerable and overwhelmed by the experience.

4 Effective support to parent and child foster carers

It is not surprising to find a number of the studies highlighting the importance of providing the foster carers with good support from both their supervising social worker, but also from the child's social worker. The Brent SCR notes that while the fostering social worker provided consistent input and support to the foster carer, there was an inconsistent level of support from the child's social worker. The report highlights that the foster carer should have been given more formal assistance in addressing the needs of the two young mothers and their babies. This mirrors a point made elsewhere (Donnelly and Wright, 2009; Greenaway, 2010; Adams and Bevan, 2011, Brent SCR) about the central role of the child's social worker in these arrangements, the importance of good communication with them, and the importance, wherever possible, of ensuring that this worker is consistent for the duration of the stay.

The research also highlighted the need for effective training. This is very clear in the serious case reviews which suggested that additional guidance was needed for social workers in relation to assessing carers for mother and child arrangements. Training needs for foster carers were identified as particularly important, including matching, recording and child protection.

5 Multi-agency working and wider support

The contribution of good multi-agency working to achieving positive outcomes is another recurrent theme. Multi-agency working matters at all stages of the process, and the Donnelly and Wright (2009) report highlights the importance of health professionals working closely with children's social care services in parent and child fostering. This indicates the benefit of a core training programme for social workers and health visitors on the role of parent and child arrangements. This recommendation is made by both the Bromley and Brent SCRs.

Issues about transitional arrangements are also discussed (Donnelly and Wright, 2009; Adams and Bevan, 2011) with an emphasis on arranging both appropriate semi-independent living, housing and good post-arrangement support. Studies note the benefits of foster carers being involved in this support.

6 The importance of assessment

While not all of the studies look at the assessment of parents, this is central to some of the literature. Most notably, both serious case reviews emphasise the failure of assessment in the child protection context, and stress the importance of this in the context of parent and child arrangements. The Bromley SCR identified shortcomings in the assessment of risk, and found that the threshold for making a legal application was met on the grounds that B would be likely to suffer significant harm. In the Brent SCR there was a suggested requirement for a pre-birth risk assessment for all young women in care who become pregnant.

Both cases highlighted the risks of focusing too heavily on current positive parenting in the assessment without taking into account either past history or assessing likelihood of sustaining progress.

Adams and Bevan (2011) also looked at the specific issue of assessment of foster carers, and found that most of the carers in their study had not been approved specifically for this specialist task. They conclude that the fostering services in their study lacked appropriate policies and procedures in this respect.

CAUTIONARY NOTE

Notwithstanding some of the positive indicators discussed, it is important to be cautious about reaching any firm conclusions based on small-scale exploratory research. Currently there are far more questions than answers, and future research is needed to look at how parent and child fostering compares with community-based or residential assessment.

It would be useful to try and identify whether there are particular characteristics of those who will make the best use of this resource. Both of the local authority studies discussed above made efforts to identify factors that correlate with poor outcomes, but the size of their samples meant any findings were of limited value. For example, Martin and Davies (2007) highlight one contra-indicator as being mothers aged over 18, whereas Donnelly and Wright (2009), in correlating likely failure with parents under the age of 20, suggest the opposite.

There are also significant questions about how fathers fit into this discussion, as in most cases they are simply not mentioned. The fact is that relatively few men participate in parent and child arrangements, and so while it is understandable that they do not feature in the existing studies, it is important that their needs and potential role are not forgotten.

3

Types of parent and child fostering

FOSTERING MODELS

There are different parent and child fostering models, each with a distinct purpose, and suitable for different situations. Broadly, they can be defined as offering assessment arrangements, support arrangements, or holding arrangements.

Assessment arrangements

Assessment arrangements are probably the most common type of parent and child fostering arrangement, and allow for a time-defined, clearly structured assessment with clear aims and objectives, such as that offered by Pathway Care's Families First Parenting Assessment Programme (see Box 1). These arrangements are usually commissioned by local authorities or court-ordered, and will often involve adult parents who have in many cases already had children removed from their care, and where the risk is relatively high. Somerset County Council Family Assessment and Support Team have usefully indicated where such arrangements might be most appropriate (see Box 2) and an example of an assessment arrangement is given in Box 3. It is this type of arrangement that has been responsible for the increased demand for arrangements with foster carers as they offer a service that might historically have been provided in a residential setting.

BOX 1   **PATHWAY CARE – ASSESSMENT STRUCTURE**

Aims of assessment

To conclude whether or not the parent can keep the child safe and meet the child's needs to a "good-enough" standard.

Assessment period

The assessment will normally last for a period of 12 weeks but this may be extended if required. Reports provided are evidence-based, qualitative and comprehensive and are prepared to provide the local authority or the court with an expert witness statement.

Reviews

Reviews are held at two weeks, six weeks and 10 weeks and involve the local authority, CAFCASS, and other professionals working with the family. An interim report will be provided following the six-week review and a final report within two weeks of the end of the 12-week assessment.

Adapted from Families First Parenting Assessment Brochure, Pathway Care, 2010

BOX 2   **SOMERSET COUNTY COUNCIL FAMILY ASSESSMENT AND SUPPORT TEAM – CRITERIA FOR ASSESSMENT PLACEMENTS**

- The child may be subject to a court order or the Public Law Outline process has started.

- The child is believed to be unsafe at home.

- The parent is believed to be unable to provide safe care, even with daytime services.

- The parent may be unco-operative.

- Placing the parent and child together should enable clear assessment information to be gathered.

- The foster carer may be expected to provide detailed assessment records that could be used in court.

Adapted from Family Assessment and Support Team Information for Professionals leaflet, Somerset County Council, 2010

BOX 3

CASE EXAMPLE OF AN ASSESSMENT ARRANGEMENT – SOMERSET COUNTY COUNCIL FAMILY ASSESSMENT AND SUPPORT TEAM

Debbie's first child, Sally, came into Somerset's care at two months after she was admitted to hospital with a spiral fracture that medical opinion identified as a non-accidental injury. Debbie and her partner Mike both denied causing the injury and the family court concluded that one of the parents did injure Sally but they could not determine which parent. Sally remained looked after whilst children's social care explored future options for Sally's care.

Debbie became pregnant again and during the pregnancy separated from Mike. Children's social care started legal proceedings before the birth of Debbie's second child to ensure the safety of the unborn baby and the court ruled a parent and child foster placement would be the best option. The family assessment and support team received the referral and were able to offer a parent and child placement with a high level of supervision and the option of Sally joining the placement at a later date.

Debbie came to the foster placement from hospital after Jack was born. She co-operated with the placement plan and with the assessment, and the carer worked very hard to supervise Debbie and provide guidance and support. Debbie's confidence grew enormously and in a structured, supportive environment she showed she could be a really good mother.

Debbie had regular contact with Sally since she was removed from her care and over time they were able to rebuild their relationship. Sally joined her mother and Jack in placement in July 2010. Debbie is looking after both children well and the Family Assessment and Support team have begun to make plans for Debbie, Jack and Sally to move into their own home together.

The parent and child placement enabled Debbie to stay in Somerset and keep in close touch with Sally and her own mother, who has been assessed as a safe carer. The foster carer will be in a position to offer time-limited support to Debbie when she moves into her own home; this is a valued feature of the scheme.

Somerset County Council Family Assessment and Support Team, April 2011

Support arrangements

With a support arrangement, the emphasis is on supporting and helping the parent, rather than assessing them, and these arrangements will be most appropriate in situations where the risks are assessed as relatively low, and it is anticipated that the parent will continue to care for the child. These arrangements are especially valid for very young mothers where the foster carers can take on a nurturing and teaching role, prior to the mother undergoing a full assessment if required. This is a very different emphasis, and is encompassed in the descriptions of support arrangements provided by Focused Fostering Services, Somerset County Council, West Sussex County Council and Fostering People (see Boxes 4–7).

It should be acknowledged that some fostering services would argue that it is unhelpful to distinguish between support and assessment, noting that an arrangement will cover both of these at the same time, and suggesting that any effective assessment needs to take place in a supportive environment.

BOX 4   **SUPPORT PLACEMENT MODEL – FOCUSED FOSTERING SERVICES**

Foster care provides a family environment of support and nurture for a young parent and their child. It can make the difference between a young person being able to develop the skills, knowledge and confidence to successfully parent their own child...and their child entering the care system...There are specific factors that need to be considered as part of their placement strategy.

- Support and guidance in preparing for parenthood at a time when many are still developing their own maturity.

- Dealing with the changing relationship with their partner or having to accept that they will be coping alone.

- Dealing with family or intergenerational conflicts that are heightened by pregnancy and may lead to initial rejection by their own parents.

- Unresolved feelings around past abuse and childhood trauma.

- Coping with the daily demands of caring for a baby or toddler.

- Managing on welfare benefits/limited finances.

- Difficulties in accessing educational and employment opportunities.

- Fear of failing...and their child being in danger of coming into public care.

Adapted from Parent and Child Placements Policy, Focused Fostering Services, 2010.

BOX 5	**SOMERSET COUNTY COUNCIL FAMILY ASSESSMENT AND SUPPORT TEAM – CRITERIA FOR SUPPORT PLACEMENTS**

- The parent is in need of support, advice and assistance to provide safe care.
- The parent is likely to be co-operative with the plan.
- There is need for some observation and assessment.
- The foster carer is not expected to provide detailed records that could be used in court.

Adapted from Information for Professionals leaflet, Somerset County Council Family Assessment and Support Team, 2010

BOX 6	**WEST SUSSEX COUNTY COUNCIL – RATIONALE FOR SUPPORT PLACEMENTS**

'Parent and baby foster care will provide a safe and friendly environment, which will enable the parent to be supervised and supported with their baby/infant. The placement will consolidate existing parenting skills as well as improving them through support, encouragement, role modelling and training...

'Parent and baby foster care should not be treated as the primary means for assessment and training of parenting skills. The foster carer will be informing the assessment, which is the responsibility of the child's social worker.'

Adapted from Policy, Placement Preparation, Practice and Protocol document, West Sussex County Council, 2010

BOX 7	CASE EXAMPLE OF A SUPPORT PLACEMENT – FOSTERING PEOPLE

'Sophie had lived with her foster carer for over a year, and the placement came to an end when she reached 16 and wanted to return to live with her mother, a plan supported by the local authority. Three months later, Fostering People were approached by that local authority to see if Sophie could return to the placement as she was now pregnant. The second placement went ahead, and after six months the local authority decided that Sophie and her baby were ready to move to a local supported lodging scheme. There was a very positive relationship between Sophie and her foster carer, and this continued even after she left the placement. The foster carer has continued to provide support to Sophie who is doing well as a young mother.'

Information provided by Fostering People, November 2010

Holding arrangements

This is an arrangement where the parent and child live in a foster home but there is no formal assessment being undertaken and no specific plan of work to support the parent with the parenting task. Often these will be time-limited arrangements, while awaiting another arrangement, or a court listing, or to allow the local authority time to consider the most appropriate care plan. Post-assessment, a holding arrangement may be appropriate to allow time for appropriate accommodation to be sought for the parent and child.

BOX 8	HOLDING ARRANGEMENTS AT PATHWAY CARE

Pathway Care also uses holding arrangements for short periods preceding assessments, for example, when the mother is physically unwell following the baby's birth or on one occasion when it was not right to separate mother and child, but time was needed to stabilise the mother's medication.

Families First Parenting Assessment Team, Pathway Care, 2011

It is worth acknowledging the existence of "pre-birth arrangements", where the mother is either already living in the foster home or will move in prior to the birth of the child. These need to be planned and considered bearing in mind the factors discussed in this practice guide, because the arrangement is likely to become a parent and child arrangement.

Family and friends

There are mixed views about whether family and friends arrangements are appropriate and workable. Some fostering services are uncomfortable with this, but others have used it to good effect, although in practice this is probably fairly unusual. Any local authority considering such an arrangement would need to be confident that the foster carer could exercise authority, manage the parent, and prioritise the needs of the child.

Brighton and Hove has developed practice guidance which sets out the need to be aware of 'significant and long-standing tensions and conflicts between the parent and potential family and friends carer and whether these may resurface and get in the way of the parent's ability to accept and follow advice'. It highlights the importance of exploring the carer's motivation and whether they feel under an obligation to provide a arrangement. The other issue to be considered at the beginning is that if the proposal is for the family and friends carer to become the child's permanent carer, and if the arrangement is not successful, this may well present a conflict of interest for the carer and create tensions for the parent. If the child is not going to remain with the carers, they would need to be able to successfully move the child to their permanent arrangement, which is likely to be adoption.

Family and friends arrangements are not specifically discussed elsewhere in this practice guidance, although much of what is discussed remains as relevant to these arrangements as it does to stranger parent and child foster carers.

SERVICE MODELS

There are two basic ways in which local authorities and independent fostering services have chosen to deliver parent and child fostering, and these can be set out as follows.

Within existing fostering services

The reality for some services is that parent and child arrangements have emerged in an ad hoc way, with carers finding themselves caring for parents and children because of circumstances, such as a young person in placement having become pregnant. Similarly, requirements to offer such an arrangement can arise from court hearings, and result in a service looking to identify a suitable resource from within their provision, even though a carer may not have initially been approved with parent and child fostering in mind.

Other services have specific carers within their numbers who have been identified as suitable for parent and child arrangements and are happy to consider these when required. Where parent and child foster carers are situated in existing fostering services, it is likely that both the foster carers and supervising social workers will also be working with other types of placements, and may need to work hard to ensure that with a parent and child arrangement they actively address all of the specific issues that need to be considered.

Specialist approach

Other local authorities or independent fostering agencies have responded to the increased demand in this area, and have developed specialist teams to offer parent and child arrangements. These are all constructed with slight differences, but have the advantage of working specifically with this client group, and as such have developed policies, procedures and practices that maximise the chances of success (see Boxes 9.1–9.3 and Box 1 at the start of this chapter).

BOX 9   **EXAMPLES OF SPECIALIST SERVICES**

9.1 Somerset County Council – Family Assessment and Support Team

In 2009, Somerset County Council set up a Family Assessment and Support Team consisting of a team leader, supervising social worker, assessing social worker, fostering support worker, and an administrator, with the remit of expanding and improving parent and child fostering. The team recruited and trained a number of foster carers to specifically work with parents and children and have developed an expertise in this area.

Adapted from Family Assessment and Support Team Information for Professionals leaflet, Somerset County Council, 2010

9.2 Brighton and Hove City Council Fostering and Adoption Service – Parent and child fostering placements

Within the fostering and adoption service in Brighton and Hove, the recruitment of prospective parent and child foster carers is profiled as a key priority. A Practice Manager within the service takes a lead role in relation to parent and child placements and she has responsibility for working with the supervising social workers to co-ordinate support and training to carers and assisting in the review and development of policies and procedures.

A dedicated support and training group is facilitated for parent and child carers which enables carers to network and access peer support as well as receive additional training input from key professionals. A range of practice guidance and resource information is available for parent and child carers as part of a specific section within the foster carers' online handbook. Additional support and input to carers is provided from the Children in Care Health Team and the Consultant Nurse in the team and Head of Fostering and Adoption undertook a piece of evaluation work on outcomes in parent and child placements, which has led to a range of practice developments, including the development of a dedicated parenting assessment programme.

Information provided by Brighton and Hove Adoption and Fostering Service, May 2011

9.3 Leeds City Council – Child and Parent Assessment Fostering Scheme

The Child and Parent Assessment Fostering Scheme was established around six years ago. Several of the foster carers providing these placements were existing carers with a specific interest in providing placements for young mothers and their children, others have a health care background within nursing, midwifery, the teaching profession and individuals who have experience of working within social care.

Those who wish to become child and parent assessment foster carers are assessed using the BAAF Form F where additional competencies that relate to the specific tasks of assessing parents need to meet. All child and parent foster carers are approved as Level 4 professional carers.

There are currently 10 approved child and parent assessment foster carers who provide assessments both in the foster home and in the community. They are supervised and supported by the principal case worker. There are no specific age restrictions both in respect of the parents or the children. However, there is a stringent matching process in place prior to consideration of a placement.

Prior to an assessment placement, social workers are required to complete a comprehensive referral form which comes directly to the principal case worker for consideration and discussion with the foster carers. A planning meeting is then held at the foster carer's home with the foster carers, parent/s, social worker and any other relevant professionals or family member attending.

The majority of assessment placements are requested prior to the birth of the child and in some situations the expectant mother moves into the placement during the latter stages of her pregnancy. However, it is typically the case that parent and child move into placement after they are discharged from hospital following the birth.

The foster carers undertake 12-week assessments with parents, although consideration can be given to these assessments being extended depending on circumstances. The progress of the assessment is reviewed regularly – every three/four weeks, with all relevant professionals and parents involved.

Information provided by Child and Parent Assessment Fostering Scheme, Leeds City Council, May 2011

4

Assessment and approval

In the past, where foster carers have historically provided parent and child arrangements, in many or most cases (Adams and Bevan, 2011) these arrangements were a response to a particular set of circumstances rather than as the result of planning to do this type of fostering. This meant that foster carers were often not assessed or approved specifically for this task. With an increasing recognition of the specific challenges of parent and child fostering, a number of fostering services have developed more specific assessment of potential carers, and there are now numerous examples of good practice in this area.

WHAT QUALITIES ARE SPECIFICALLY REQUIRED FOR PARENT AND CHILD FOSTER CARERS?

This is the key question, as any assessment needs to be undertaken in the context of knowing what is required. It is clear that parent and child carers need all the personal attributes needed by other foster carers of both babies and young people. In any assessment it is important that these are thoroughly considered, and cover all the recognised competencies needed by foster carers. This will include considering the suitability of the accommodation for the task in hand, and the applicants understanding what is entailed in being a foster carer. However, in certain respects parent and child carers need an additional knowledge and skill set, and in some areas may need an extra level of ability on top of what is required for other foster carers. These key additional qualities are set out below.

Ability to accept "good enough" parenting

A crucial element in parent and child fostering is the fact that the foster carer is not the primary carer for the child (usually a baby), and this responsibility lies with the child's parent or parents. This means that the foster carer, rather than providing direct care, is required to observe, support and facilitate the parent in providing this. When people become foster carers, they do so because they want to look after children, and want to do what is best for them. Parents who require parent and child fostering arrangements – certainly assessment arrangements – are by definition likely to be struggling to provide even "good enough" care. For a foster carer, the challenge is to allow the parent to struggle to establish "good enough" parenting for their child, even if this conflicts with the foster carer's views about what they think is good parenting. Some people will be able to manage this very different role to that usually associated with being a foster carer. For others, observing parenting that is just about adequate might be too painful for them to bear. To be effective, parent and child foster carers will need to be able to manage their own feelings and emotions, and approach their task in a non-judgmental manner. At times, parent and child carers will also be required to demonstrate particularly strong advocacy skills, using these to either put the parent's case, or speak on behalf of the child.

Child protection awareness

Linked to this, parent and child foster carers will have a particular remit to ensure the safety of children in their homes. But these children continue to be cared for by parents who local authorities have assessed as not being able to care for their children in a normal community setting. This might not be an easy task, as carers need to make calm and objective judgments about what is safe care and what is not. In order to do this, it is crucial that they have a good understanding of child development, and up-to-date practical knowledge about caring for young children. Carers will also need the confidence to know when to step in, when to contact other professionals for advice and guidance, and at times they will need to be assertive in managing parental responses that pose a risk to the child.

Working with birth parents

While all foster carers need to be able to work effectively with birth parents, for most of them this is not in the context of the parents living in their homes. With parent and child fostering, the relationship between the foster carer and the parent is particularly crucial, and the carers will need to find an appropriate balance between keeping professional boundaries, but also being warm and supportive. They may also need to be able to support contact arrangements, where agreed as taking place in the foster home.

Given the context in which these arrangements are often set up and their remit, it is necessary for the carer to have particularly strong communication and relationship-building skills. It is not easy for anxious or angry parents to take advice and guidance about their parenting, particularly when they know they are being observed and assessed. Effective parent and child carers will need to be able to teach patiently, criticise constructively without demoralising, be able to offer praise without being perceived as patronising, and model good parenting. They will need to be able to judge when it is appropriate to say something, and when it might be better to allow some space, and create an appropriate balance between encouraging parents without misleading them into thinking their care is "good enough" if it is not.

All of this requires a sensitive, nurturing and calm personality, combined with good judgment and a willingness to make use of professional support. It is likely that parent and child foster carers will be subjected to parents questioning and challenging their own family life. If this happens, they will need to be emotionally robust and well supported sufficiently to deal with this.

Keeping written records and contributing to assessments

All foster carers need to be able to keep records, but recording in parent and child fostering is more demanding because of the specific nature of the task. In assessment arrangements, foster care records will be used to inform assessment reports, and it is possible that they may be used in care proceedings in reaching hugely significant decisions about the future of a child. This means that parent and child foster carers need to be able to record clearly and accurately, making a distinction between fact and opinion. They may also need to give evidence in court about their records and about wider matters. It is important that they are able to do this with appropriate preparation and support.

Practical considerations

Given that parent and child arrangements often involve the foster carer sharing their home with another adult, the issue of space is particularly important. It can be challenging, for example, if the home is not spacious enough to allow at least two people to use the kitchen simultaneously or for parents to have access to lounge space to spend time with their child away from the carer and others in the foster family. The requirement for "private space" and time needs to be managed alongside the need for high levels of supervision and observation, and so while a self-contained area within the property might be appropriate in some cases, this needs to be considered alongside the need to meet other objectives in the arrangement. There may also be other practical aspects to consider, such as whether the carer is expected to be in the home at all times, and if so, how this can be managed.

The assessment format

Most fostering services will use either the BAAF Form F or the Fostering Network form for undertaking assessments of foster carers. These are also suitable for parent and child foster carers, with some additional work. Chapman (2009) has identified some particular additional questions that can be used (See Box 10 below), and some fostering services such as Foster Care Associates and Leeds Social Care have produced additional competencies to be addressed when considering parent and child foster carers (see Box 11 and Appendix 2). TACT has also developed a specific addendum form that covers the areas discussed above (see Appendix 3).

BOX 10   **ADDITIONAL AREAS TO COVER FOR PARENT AND BABY APPLICATIONS**

- Have the applicants got the time and space for this kind of fostering?

- What is the applicant's understanding of what this kind of placement involves?

- What do they feel will be the rewards for them?

- What is their understanding of what constitutes "good enough" parenting?

- How would they decide when to get involved with the care of the baby and when to step back?

- Could the applicants provide an appropriate level of supervision to ensure the safety of the baby is paramount at all times?

- Has the applicant the ability to make a detailed assessment of the quality of care offered by the parent?

- Has the applicant the ability to write sound, evidence-based reports?

- Are they prepared for the possibility that they may have to give evidence in court?

- How able would the applicant be to work with a wide range of other professionals?

- Does the applicant understand the implications of having, potentially, another adult living in their home?

- Do they understand the implications for this kind of placement on the individual members of their household?

Chapman R (2009) Undertaking a Fostering Assessment, BAAF: London.

> ## BOX 11   FOSTER CARE ASSOCIATES – ASSESSMENT CRITERIA
>
> 5.   Caring for parents and their children
>
> 5.1   An ability to provide support, guidance and training to the parent in assessment in order to assist the development of parenting and independent living skills, but also to be able to remain objective and not compromise the assessor's role.
>
> 5.2   An ability to ensure that a parental assessment remains sensitive to the parent's own culture and values.
>
> 5.3   An ability to understand the impact of past experiences, current stresses and levels of learning impairment on a person's capacity to develop parenting skills.
>
> 5.4   An ability to provide adequate and appropriate levels of supervision to ensure that the safety of the child remains paramount at all times.
>
> 5.5   An ability to produce factual daily records and weekly summaries, which are evidentially sound, and to share these with the parent in placement.
>
> 5.6   An ability to write or contribute to the writing of assessment reports for court.
>
> *Extract from the Extra Competency Matrix for Parent and Child Approval, Foster Care Associates, 2010*

DO PARENT AND CHILD FOSTER CARERS NEED OTHER FOSTERING EXPERIENCE PRIOR TO UNDERTAKING THIS ROLE?

The question of what level of prior experience is needed as a foster carer before moving onto this particular specialist area is an important one. There is one argument that says that because fostering is different from any other type of child care work, in that it takes place in the person's own home 24 hours a day, it is difficult to predict how this will feel without having experienced it. Furthermore, one of the challenges for foster carers is getting used to being in a position where they provide day-to-day "parenting" and yet do not hold parental responsibility and are part of a professional team. Even for people with significant experience with children and young people, this particular role can be challenging, and can take some getting used to. This suggests that there might be advantages for people in first gaining experience of mainstream fostering before adding the specific challenges that come with parent and child arrangements.

While for many people that might be the right approach, it must be recognised that setting this as a blanket requirement might not be helpful. Some potential carers might have particular experiences or skills that make them want to undertake this specific role. Adams and Bevan (2011, p. 34) interviewed such a foster carer:

> When my youngest two were in their teens they said, 'We have spare rooms, why don't we foster?', and I said, 'No, when you've all grown up then I will'. Then my youngest child got pregnant...we were both shocked at how much support she needed as she was used to looking after children. She said, 'If I need so much help with all the interaction I've had with babies and children, then think how hard it is for other young mums,' and she suggested I do mother and baby fostering.

Some fostering services have experience of recruiting potential foster carers with backgrounds in residential settings, social work, or paediatrics, who may be fully aware of the fostering role, and who are particularly committed to parent and child fostering, and would have the transferable skills to do this to a high standard. It has also been argued that existing foster carers have established practices and expectations and may have to "unlearn" these to be successful parent and child foster carers. For example, carers who have not fostered before might have less difficulty in standing back and letting parents manage the child care tasks, rather than taking the lead role. Some fostering services report that many of their best parent and child foster carers have never fostered previously. This suggests that every applicant should be assessed for their particular strengths and experiences bearing in mind the specific demands of being a parent and child foster carer.

SHOULD PARENT AND CHILD FOSTER CARERS HAVE OTHER CHILDREN IN THEIR HOUSEHOLD?

Given the issues involved in providing parent and child foster arrangements, some services have taken the view that it is not appropriate for carers to be fostering other children at the same time. There are two key factors that need to be considered: safety and time.

As noted in the legal section, an adult parent is considered a member of the fostering household. However, by definition they will have had difficulties in parenting their child adequately, and in practice may not have completed a CRB check before moving in. Services will need to have a safeguarding policy that ensures the safety of any other child where a parent (of a parent and child arrangement) is living in the foster home. In addition to ensuring that any foster child will not be at risk of abuse from a parent, it will also be necessary to consider the risk of a child being re-traumatised by witnessing another child being poorly parented. For example, a parent shouting at their toddler, or not responding appropriately to a baby in distress, might be difficult for another foster child if they are sensitive to shouting because of past experiences, or if this reminds them of being witness to domestic violence, or if they have been responsible for caring for younger siblings.

On the other hand, another child could potentially join a household with a very settled parent and child arrangement, or it may be that the parent is a teenager who could be younger than the other child placed. It could be argued that with careful identification of the risks and advantages, having a parent and child living in the foster home presents no greater risk than a regular fostering arrangement.

There is also evidence that teenage birth children can be positive role models for young parents, and that birth children's feedback to the parent can at times be better received than feedback from the carer in the assessor role. The presence of other children in the household may help the parent to feel that they are part of a "real family" for the first time and the presence of birth children in the household allows the parent to witness examples of positive parenting in action which could be more effective than spoken advice. However, whilst parents can get tremendous benefit from seeing the carer parent or observing how disagreement is resolved, they cannot be "part of the carer's family" and making them so in the short term may make the loss all the greater when they need to leave.

One mother, when asked for feedback of her experience, made many positive comments about how welcome she had felt, how much she had learnt and so on before saying that the bad thing was 'being given a family then having it taken away'. Workers therefore will need to be mindful of parents who have experienced repeated loss, rejection and separation and how a further loss may impact upon them.

The other factor to consider is whether the foster carer has enough time to adequately meet the needs of another child placed alongside that of the parent and child. As discussed above, the demands of a parent and child arrangement can be high, and it is important that neither this parent and child, or another child placed, suffers as the result of the presence of the other in the foster home. This was particularly highlighted in the Brent SCR where there was more than one parent and child arrangement in the household. These situations should be subject to an appropriate risk assessment. Against that argument, it should be recognised that some fostering households – particularly if there are two full-time carers – may have the capacity to manage some very demanding arrangements. An arbitrary limit may not be the most helpful approach, but rather that each case should be assessed on its merits.

Whatever policy the fostering service arrives at in this respect, it is essential that they fully take account of both the safety issues as well as the time commitment that a parent and child arrangement will demand.

In considering these issues, the fostering service will need to consider whether their policy should cover the issue of birth children, and whether or not there should be any limits on carers with birth children at home being in a position to undertake parent and child fostering. Clearly the age of the child would be an important factor, as it might be deemed too difficult for the carer to be parenting their own baby or infant, but might work well if the child is older. Again, the fostering service would need to consider safety issues and time commitments. Whatever policy a service establishes, it is important to consider that there could be potential benefits to parents being able to see foster carers role modelling appropriate parenting.

Outlook Fostering has considered these issues and their policy statement is included in Box 12.

BOX 12   **OUTLOOK FOSTERING SERVICES' POLICY STATEMENT ON OTHER CHILDREN**

- Some may have children at home, others may not, although if carers have children of their own it works best if there are two carers, to ensure that carers' own children's needs can be met.

- It is not generally recommended that a parent/child placement is placed alongside foster children, primarily because the parent/child assessment usually involves a very high level of supervision and the parent may potentially pose a threat to the child.

- With more settled longer-term placements, it may be possible to match a fostered child alongside a parent and child.

Extract from Outlook Fostering Services Ltd, Parent and Child Assessment Placements: Guidance for carers and staff, 2010.

APPROVAL TERMS AND THE FOSTERING PANEL

This is a difficult area to navigate, particularly given that in England a foster carer is a person approved and assessed in the context of their suitability to foster. Therefore, the panel process and any agreed terms of approval relate to their suitability as a foster carer and not any other activity or arrangements they are involved in.

In England, the fostering service provider is required to carry out an assessment of prospective foster carers and compile a written report that includes matters prescribed in the Fostering Services (England) Regulations 2011, including any other information the fostering service provider considers relevant.

Such other information could include, for example, how their skills and experience could also be relevant to their suitability to provide parent and child arrangements and support parenting assessment in the context of their approval as a foster carer.

The following are some clear good practice principles that can be applied when deciding on terms of approval for foster carers involved in parent and child arrangements.

- It is appropriate that fostering services consider the fostering household's suitability specifically for the parent and child arrangements where they intend their foster carers to be used for this activity. Even if a foster carer is approved to care for children aged 0–18, this is unlikely to adequately cover the skills and capabilities needed for the parent and child arrangements without specific consideration.

- With this in mind, it is important that fostering panels are trained to understand the specific challenges for foster carers involved in parent and child arrangements so that they can effectively scrutinise such applications.

- If a service thinks it is appropriate for a foster carer to care for more than one parent and child at the same time, or alongside the placement of a looked after child, then careful consideration will be needed about how this might work in practice and how the terms of approval are worded in the context of caring for a parent and child.

- In England, fostering services also need to be mindful of the fact that not all arrangements are placements (involve looked after children), and to ensure that the wording of the approval clearly reflects what is intended.

While there are arguments to suggest that "terms of approval" are not the right mechanism for managing activity that is technically outside of fostering, it is important that fostering panels (and fostering services) do clearly indicate what they consider is an appropriate level of commitment for any particular household where they are being approved to foster. Whether these are parent and child placements or arrangements that are not placements, is often a legal distinction that means little in terms of whether the foster carers can meet the needs of the specific parents and their children.

So, it is not within the remit of fostering panels to recommend the approval of foster carers for arrangements that are not placements, but they can give advice to fostering services, and there are strong arguments for suggesting that any recommendations for approval are accompanied by advice which covers arrangements that are not placements. Fostering panels may want to use phrases like:

Recommendation:

Mr and Mrs X should be approved as foster carers for one parent and child placement.

Mr and Mrs X should be approved as foster carers for two parent and child placements subject to not exceeding the usual fostering limit.

Mr and Mrs X should be approved as foster carers for one parent and child placement, and as task-centred foster carers for one child aged 11–18 of either sex.

Mr and Mrs X should be approved as task-centred foster carers for three children aged 0–18 of either sex, or as foster carers for one parent and child placement.

Advice:

This recommendation should be taken into account when considering a parent and child arrangement which is not a placement.

USUAL FOSTERING LIMIT

It is worth bearing in mind that the usual fostering limit[5] is three. This means that no one may foster more than three children unless: the foster children are all siblings in relation to each other (in which case there is no upper limit), or the local authority within whose area the foster carer lives exempts the foster carer from the usual fostering limit in relation to specific placements.

A child who is not looked after does not count towards the usual fostering limit, but if they are part of a parent and child arrangement in the household, then good practice would indicate that this needs to be taken into account when making judgements about what is appropriate and deciding whether to grant an exemption from the usual fostering limit.

5   Schedule 7 to the Children Act 1989 limits the number of children who may be fostered by a foster carer. The "usual fostering limit" is set at three.

5

Training and supporting foster carers

All foster carers who are offering parent and child arrangements will need to receive all the core training required by mainstream foster carers. They will also need additional training to meet the specific demands of this type of arrangement.

Where fostering services are recruiting to specific schemes, they are likely to incorporate and target such training into the training offered to carers from the point of preparation for their fostering role. For other carers who are transferring to the role or offering such arrangements within their terms of approval, training will need to be offered as part of their ongoing training needs.

Training should be available for both the principal carer and their partner (where applicable) and it may be appropriate for a single carer to be accompanied by their support carer. Some fostering services have made attendance for both carers mandatory. Where they have not, fostering services should consider whether at least some sessions should require the attendance of both carers. Other fostering services have encouraged the supervising social worker to attend the training with the carers.

A number of fostering services have developed in-house pre- and post-approval training courses for carers which range from two-day to seven-day courses, as shown in Box 13.

Fostering services have used practitioners from other disciplines to deliver specific training, e.g. a health visitor to deliver training on child development. Where resources are not available or there are small numbers of carers, services could consider sharing training with another fostering service or making use of appropriate external courses.

BOX 13   **PRACTICE EXAMPLES OF TRAINING COURSES**

The Adolescent and Children's Trust (TACT) has developed a seven-day training course for their parent and child foster carers and are seeking to get the course accredited as a diploma or certificate (see Appendix 4).

Somerset County Council has used a specialist midwife to help understand the impact of alcohol and substance abuse on parenting and the impact of alcohol and drugs during pregnancy and birth. A clinical psychologist has provided advice on working with and assessing parents with learning disabilities.

Team Fostering offers a Family Links Nurturing Programme, a structured 10-session programme promoting emotional health, relationship skills and positive behaviour management strategies for parents/carers, which has been accredited. This programme encourages an approach to relationships that gives children and parents an emotionally healthy springboard for their lives and their learning. It has a multi-fold aim of:

- promoting emotional literacy and emotional health;

- enhancing self-esteem, self-awareness and empathy;

- developing communication and relationship skills;

- providing effective strategies to encourage co-operative, responsible behaviour and manage challenging behaviour in children.

ISP Rainham provides a "Sign Along" course to foster carers involved in parent and child placements to enable them to communicate more efficiently with children with no or limited vocabulary. They have also widened this out to include the parents and had three parents attend alongside foster carers in a group training session. The training was well received by all who attended and foster carers reported that they observed the parents who attended the course putting into practice what they had learnt.

The suggested range of training needs identified specifically for parent/child carers includes the following:

- the day-to-day reality of fostering a parent and child (ideally with the input of experienced parent/child carers);

- child development, paediatric first aid and the care needs of babies;

- building positive relationships with parents including empowerment and advocacy;

- working with birth parents to promote nurturing parenting;

- an understanding of attachment and how to promote good attachments;
- working with parents with a physical or learning disability, mental health problems or a history of self-harm;
- risk assessment and how to manage risk;
- child protection and safeguarding, including signs of abuse;
- safe caring in the home for parent and child arrangements;
- the legal context of parent and child arrangements;
- undertaking assessments and use of assessment tools;
- recording, report writing, court skills and giving evidence in court.

As with any training for foster carers, this is best delivered using a variety of methods including presentations, large group discussions and small task-focused group work, using tools such as video material or case studies with experienced parent and child foster carers being included as presenters or being available to share their experiences.

Fostering services need to ensure that they make arrangements for their carers to attend training during the period of the arrangement if the parent cannot be left unattended. This may mean arranging attendance at a family centre or providing appropriately trained respite carers such as sessional workers or other parent and child carers in order for the carers to be able to attend.

Following the training, it should be understood that feedback will be shared with the carer's supervising social worker to enable further discussion to address any outstanding issues specific to the carers and their family situation or to identify further development or training needs.

SUPPORT

Parent and child arrangements involve complex and challenging issues for carers and they need to receive a high level of support. Many fostering services offer weekly visits from the supervising social worker to the foster carer at least initially and in some schemes for the duration of the arrangement. Where visits are agreed with the carer at a less frequent level once the arrangement is more established, this needs to be kept under review with the carer in order to respond to any changes or developments. These visits will include discussion about the care being offered by the parent, helping the carer with recording or using assessment tools, reviewing how the arrangement is going and giving the carer the opportunity to express any concerns about the impact of the arrangement on them or other members of their household.

It is important for the role of these visits to be clear – are they for support or for formal supervision of the carers? Do they include more formal meetings such as planning for arrangements or review meetings? Recording the content of the supervision will provide evidence of the carer's competencies and help clarify both the carer's and supervising social worker's roles. Fostering services may also undertake unannounced visits to the foster carer but these should be seen as additional to the regular supervisory visits.

Further support will also be provided through foster carer support groups and, where possible, carers will benefit from attending groups specifically set up for parent and child carers. These can be used both for discussion and support and for additional training opportunities such as having speakers to explore specific topics not covered in initial training or perhaps responding to an identified need. Other opportunities can be offered such as mentoring or buddying by experienced parent and child carers, particularly for new carers offering these arrangements as well as encouraging carers to use other informal support networks.

Valuable support can be provided by other professionals, particularly health professionals, when looking at specific issues relating to the care of the baby/child. However, there should be co-ordination of such advice so that the foster carer does not find themselves or the parents receiving conflicting or contradictory advice from different professionals. It is important for the supervising social worker to monitor this.

BOX 14   **HEALTH VISITORS AT PATHWAY CARE**

Health visitors play an important role in assessments at Pathway Care. It is an expectation that parents will make and keep regular health visitor appointments. During the initial stages the parent will often spend some time alone with the health visitor but then at the end, the carer will be invited in so that the parent can explain to the carer any advice that the health visitor has given. This offers an opportunity for the carer to ask further questions, the health visitor to explain in more depth, and an assessment of the parent's understanding to be carried out.

Families First Parenting Assessment Team, Pathway Care, 2011

Parent and child arrangements are by their nature likely to create particular stresses and times of crisis, with carers providing 24-hour observation, supervision and support. For this reason they should have access to 24-hour support, ideally not just through an emergency duty team in the placing local authority but through their approving fostering service. It has also been suggested that it would be good practice that in each arrangement the supervising social worker has a named manager or co-worker who is also familiar with the arrangement to offer support in their social worker's absence.

For foster carers who are providing time-limited assessed arrangements, for example, fixed period assessments of up to three months, there is usually no formal respite provision or opportunities for holidays to be taken by carers. Fostering services need to think creatively about how to provide appropriate breaks during these periods, for example, developing a pool of respite parent/child carers.

BOX 15   **PRACTICE EXAMPLES OF SUPPORT FOR PARENT AND CHILD FOSTER CARERS**

Southampton Council has introduced group supervision of their parent and child carers together with support workers in order to promote the sharing of good practice.

Brighton and Hove parent and baby carers have developed skill-sharing between carers and built up a library of resources for new carers.

Pathway Care has a monthly Parenting Assessment Carer Support Group meeting. The first part of the meeting is used for the staff and carers to share any new information, policies and procedures and to discuss any issues that have arisen in the working relationship between carers and office-based staff. The second part of the meeting is for carers to discuss and explore with a consultant psychologist any practice or management issues arising from their placements.

SAFER CARING

Having a good understanding of safer caring principles is crucial for all foster carers. This might be deemed particularly important when another adult, often a young woman, is joining a household that includes a male carer or other adult males. This is something that is addressed very thoroughly by the Foster Care Co-operative and Outlook Fostering (see Boxes 16 and 17).

Furthermore, there is an increasing risk of an allegation being made if the assessment is not going well. Parents may feel desperate and that they need to give themselves another chance in a different setting. Foster carers need to think very carefully about how they are going to manage issues like this, and require support and training from their fostering service. The fostering service should have a policy about how they manage allegations made against carers that also considers the importance of not destabilising any other children who are in placement with the foster carer.

BOX 16 **SAFE CARE MODULE – FOSTER CARE CO-OPERATIVE**

Foster Care Co-operative separates the course participants on their Safe Care module into male and female groups. They have found that although these groups identify some similar issues, it is the differences raised between the groups that provide the main points for further work with the applicants.

The men have identified issues such as being left alone in the home with the young parent and whether "mates" can still come round to watch football and have a beer; what level of involvement they should have with a young parent, e.g. taking them out to appointments; and how they should deal with a young parent making advances towards them. Other issues relate to their own relationship as a couple needing "private time" and the impact on their family life.

The women have identified issues such as practical issues of time management; undertaking everyday tasks in the home whilst monitoring the parent/child; what changes are needed to their current family safe care policy; and additional equipment needs; but also concerns about a male partner or adult/teenage sons being left alone in the home and how to protect them, whether their children can have friends over, and ensuring confidentiality is maintained for all parties.

Adapted from information provided by Foster Care Co-operative, February 2011.

BOX 17   **SAFER CARING FAMILY POLICY – OUTLOOK FOSTERING**

Before or on the same day of the placement, Outlook ensures that the foster carer and LA social worker have a draft safer caring family policy to consider. Sometimes, when placements are dealt with on an emergency basis, a placement agreement meeting does not take place until some days later. However, the SCFP ensures that the foster carer and parent are clear about important safe care issues/arrangements as soon as the placement has been made.

The "draft" SCFP includes the following guidance:

- Pets – Parent to ensure that a baby/child is never left unattended with any of the pets. If the baby needs to be left alone in a room (for example, when he is asleep in his Moses basket), then the parent needs to close the door and use the baby monitor.

- Parent may not disclose the current address to any of her family members/ friends.

- Parent is not allowed to take baby out of the placement unsupervised.

- Parent can be left unsupervised for short periods of time at the carer's home; up to half an hour.

- Parent should not allow baby to sleep in bed with her.

- This SCFP will be regularly reviewed in partnership with the LA social worker; emails will confirm revised arrangements.

Adapted from information provided by Outlook Fostering, May 2011

FINANCE

Parent and child arrangements are very demanding, and as such, foster carers should receive allowances and fees that reflect the cost of having a parent and child living in the fostering household and the time, complexities and skills the foster carers need. Payment arrangements and other money matters should be agreed upon in the planning meeting prior to the start of the arrangement, and all involved should be clear about the expectations regarding payments.

Fostering services will have in place various payment options for their carers. Some fostering services are paying carers allowances to cover the costs of caring for both the parent (regardless of the age of the parent) and the child, and/or a fee for the assessment of the parent and the child. This may depend on whether the arrangement is seen as providing support or assessment, and the allowance paid for the parent may be reduced if the parent is able to receive child benefit or income support. Other fostering services are only making one payment to the carer that may, for example, reflect a single arrangement or one-and-a-half times the usual fostering fee. Some fostering services have used a bonus scheme payment for foster carers at the end of the year or after completing a set number of arrangements.

While there will be a number of equally valid payment schemes, there needs to be clarity about all aspects of payments. This should cover issues such as whether the foster carer or the parent receives child benefit for the child and who pays for the child's expenses. In some cases, the practice is for the carer to receive child benefit and pass this on to the parent for them to pay for the child's expenses. In others, the parent receives the child benefit directly, with an expectation that they spend it on their child. Where money is given directly to the parent, they may be encouraged to save this to provide for future accommodation, or to support the baby. This is also an area where the carer may find themselves making value judgements about what is a good use of money and what is not, so there needs to be guidance for the carer on the service's expectations. This will need to include a view on how much independence should be given to the parent, for example, in deciding whether to buy new or second-hand clothes for the child.

Advice on benefits can be easily accessed on the Direct Gov website at www.direct.gov.uk/en/MoneyTaxAndBenefits/BenefitsTaxCreditsAndOtherSupport/Expectingorbringingupchildren/index.htm.

There may also be implications for any benefit entitlements of the carer; these will depend on whether one or both of the parent and child are considered to be a looked after child.

Fostering providers have highlighted that there may be issues for parents in relation to any housing benefits they claim, for example, depending on the length of time the parents are living in the foster home, parents might find they lose their entitlement to these. It is therefore important that discussions are held with the relevant agencies prior to any arrangement being made.

If the carer is living in social housing, an adult parent could be classed as a lodger and may have to pay council tax. These issues need to be fully explored by the service and the carer prior to any arrangements being made.

There is information available on the HMRC website about how arrangements of parents under 18 with children who are not looked after will be viewed (see www.hmrc.gov.uk/individuals/foster-carers.htm#h). This does not cover the other variations of legal status that can occur and it is important that foster carers seek clarification about whether the elements of their payments relating to adults will need to be declared separately.

6

Care planning and placement planning

While fostering arrangements are often made in situations characterised by crisis and urgency, it is generally recognised that time invested in planning prior to the arrangement can be crucial in maximising the chances of the arrangement working well and achieving the desired outcomes (Adams and Bevan, 2011; Donnelly and Wright, 2009; Greenaway, 2010). In some cases, parent and child arrangements are made in circumstances in which planning opportunities are limited. It is important in these circumstances to remember that lack of clarity about roles and responsibilities is a significant factor when things have gone wrong. It is therefore essential that placing social workers and fostering services invest time and effort into getting the planning right, as this provides a good foundation for everything that follows.

Where possible, this should include strategic planning as required under the "sufficiency duty". Local authorities are expected to have arrangements in place to meet the needs of their care population, and increasingly this must include a need for parent and child arrangements. Some local authorities will achieve this through an in-house fostering service (see Box 18 describing arrangements in Somerset County Council), and others will do this by having service level agreements or spot purchasing from independent fostering agencies. Whatever the approach, the aim must be to look at care planning for parent and child arrangements both on an individual case by case basis, but also in their strategic plans.

BOX 18	SOMERSET COUNTY COUNCIL CARE PLANNING

In Somerset there is a dedicated parent and child team that works closely with childcare social workers to strategically plan ahead. The manager of that team notes that it is possible to plan placements two or three months prior to birth, so that in November, for example, placements are being finalised ready for December or January.

However, some arrangements will be made at short notice where perhaps the local authority has gone to court with a care plan for separation that was not agreed and has then had to identify an arrangement at short notice. Some parents may not accept the potential plan for a parent and child foster arrangement until after the baby is born and the realities of the local authority care plan become evident. In these situations, it is difficult to undertake much planning but every attempt should be made for the foster carer to at least meet the parent prior to the parent arriving at their house.

BOX 19   **BRIGHTON AND HOVE CITY COUNCIL ADOPTION AND FOSTERING SERVICE – EARLY PERMANENCE TEAM**

Brighton and Hove City Council is in the process of developing an early permanence team staffed by specialist health visitors and early years visitors, with consultation from experienced social work practitioners from the service's assessment centre. The aim of this team is to get involved in some pre-birth assessment work with vulnerable families where it is identified that a baby is at risk of care proceedings or there is a child protection plan in place at birth. This team would also undertake assessment/parenting skills work post-birth in an assessment plan overseen by the child's social worker.

ASSESSING THE SUITABILITY OF THE PARENT FOR A PARENT AND CHILD ARRANGEMENT

The first question to consider must be whether a particular parent and child have been assessed as suitable to live together in a fostering environment. This will be informed by a variety of factors. In relation to support arrangements, there will need to be evidence to suggest that a parent is likely to be able to effectively parent their child, be able to accept support, and be willing to do this in the context of a foster home. For an assessment arrangement, it will need to be established that the parent is willing to participate in such an assessment, and that the risks to any child are such that they can safely be managed in the context of a foster home.

It is clearly the responsibility of the fostering service – as well as any commissioning local authority – to be satisfied that any arrangement is appropriate, and that the foster carer is well placed to meet the various requirements of the arrangement. This may involve them undertaking a specific assessment of the potential parent and child, or they may rely on the child's social worker to do this. In either event, the planning process will effectively start with a referral or placement request.

Referral or request for a parent and child arrangement

The first step in considering a parent's suitability will be to request a referral from the child's social worker (or other professional) that will provide information about the parent and child, and the reason why a parent and child arrangement has been requested. Specific information will be required about a range of basic matters pertaining to both the parent and child, and the wider planning context of the arrangement:

- names and contact details for all key persons including professionals and the parent and child;

- basic details including age, health, disability, religion, language and ethnicity;

- information about any current placement or situation;

- the short- and long-term plans, including details of any court dates that are pending;

- information about education or employment;

- views or wishes of the parent about their wishes and expectations of a parent and child arrangement;

- details of others who are to play a part in the arrangement, such as partners;

- proposed contact arrangements;

- any court directions.

Additionally, it will be necessary to get more detailed information about the particular issues that have led to the request for this particular family to move into a parent and child arrangement. Fostering People use a well set out Parent and Child Referral Form, reproduced as Appendix 5.

Where information is not made available in sufficient detail, then the onus must be on the fostering service to not accept the referral until it is available. This is not always easy, but fostering services have a duty of care to their foster carers as well as to parents and children moving into the foster home, and this must entail only accepting placements where the fostering services can meet the identified needs. If insufficient or inadequate information is provided at the referral stage, then it will not be possible to assess this with any reliability.

Risk assessment

The documentation should include a risk assessment that primarily focuses on the parent, to ensure that they will be able to live in a foster home without jeopardising the health and safety of any other household members. This is particularly important in relation to adult parents who are not used to living with foster carers, and a good risk assessment will need to consider the following factors.

- Any criminal convictions, cautions, or police involvement?

- Any history of child abuse, or abuse of animals?

- Any history of violence including domestic violence, threats of violence, or intimidating behaviour (considering any patterns of targeting one sex or the other, and any use of weapons)?

- Any history of arson or damage to property?

- Any inappropriate sexualised behaviour?

- Any history of alcohol or substance misuse?

- Any history of self-harming?

- Any history of absconding from placements?

- Any medical risks such as epilepsy, diabetes, asthma, etc?

- Any behaviour arising from mental health conditions or non-compliance about medication?

If there is evidence of any of these factors, it will be necessary to get full details and make an assessment in relation to the likelihood and severity of harm, and, if the arrangement remains viable, to look at measures to mitigate or reduce the risk. For example, where a baby is born experiencing withdrawal symptoms, and there is a need for the baby to have a high level of good quality care, a risk assessment should look at whether this would be available from a parent with their own unstable drug use. Does the parent need to focus on their own substance misuse before being able to focus on their capacity to meet the needs of the baby? Where a parent is on a controlled methadone programme, there would be a need for full consideration of how the methadone would be stored safely within the foster home and accessed by the parent.

This will obviously need to include discussions with any proposed foster carer and the responsible authority of any child placed with that carer, and must take account of the needs of others living in the fostering household. The risk assessment also should be applied to others who may play a part in the arrangement, such as partners of parents, even if they are not proposing to live in the foster home. Consideration should be given to whether the address of the foster home would be required to remain confidential. If so, a risk assessment should explore if this is possible as the mother may be under some pressure from the father of the child or her ex-partner to disclose her whereabouts.

It is important to be clear that parent and child arrangements are not appropriate for all parent and child cases. There may be issues that arise in the course of undertaking a risk assessment that indicate that a parent is not suitable to live in a foster home. Fostering services will be very aware of their duty towards foster carers, and must ensure that their safety, and the safety of their family, remains the priority.

There should be clear acknowledgements between all fostering services that, in spite of a risk assessment being undertaken at the outset, there may be previously unknown factors that emerge over the course of an arrangement. Good practice requires risk assessments to be reviewed and updated on an ongoing basis, and for action to be taken in response to any changes. At times, it may be necessary to end arrangements to ensure the safety of foster carers and others, although clearly this will be a last resort.

It is worth reflecting on the issue of domestic violence, a common factor in child protection cases. While it may be appropriate for a parent who has experienced domestic violence, usually a mother, to be offered a parent and child arrangement, this will need to be carefully considered in light of what is known about the perpetrator. Sometimes this might be most appropriate if the foster home is some geographical distance from their previous home. The foster carer should ideally be provided with a full description and photograph of the ex-partner, and it may be necessary to clearly stipulate that if the perpetrator becomes aware of the address, it will be necessary to end the arrangement. In other cases, it might be necessary to first ask the mother to move into a refuge or safe house as an interim measure, in order to demonstrate a commitment to ending the violent relationship. See Appendices 6 and 7 for documents of adult risk assessments from Pathway Care and Somerset County Council.

PREPARING BIRTH PARENTS

Having assessed a parent and child as suitable for a parent and child arrangement, it will be necessary to prepare the parent as much as possible, in order to maximise the chances of success. Parents need to know what they are agreeing to when they agree to the arrangement, and to be clear about what will be expected of them. Fostering services that regularly offer parent and child arrangements have developed information leaflets for parents (details about the contents of those from Somerset, West Sussex and Brighton and Hove are contained as Appendix 8).

While in practice it is often babies who are placed with their parents, in cases where the children are older, it is important that they too are prepared for the move, and that in-depth preparatory work is carried out with them as is best practice for all placement moves.

BOX 20   **OUTLOOK FOSTERING – WELCOMING PACKS**

Outlook Fostering sends out a "welcoming pack" to the parent and baby on the same day that a placement is made.

The pack includes:

- welcoming letter and complaints procedure
- *I'm only a baby but...* booklet (produced by Child Accident Prevention Trust) and possibly other relevant literature as deemed appropriate
- a little baby toy or a £5 voucher

Pathway Care has also developed the idea of a memory box that is given to all parents at the outset of the arrangement (see Box 21).

BOX 21   **PATHWAY CARE – MEMORY BOXES**

A memory box is given to all families at the start of any placement with Pathway Care. Inside the sturdy and brightly coloured box, we usually include a camera, photo album, photo frame, a toy and other items which will encourage the parent to think about what they would like their child to remember in the future. It sets the tone of the relationship between the fostering service and the parent, giving the parent responsibility for their child and being respectful of their wishes and feelings.

Encouraging parents to think about what they would like their child to know about their current circumstances is helpful in opening up discussions about what they recall about their own childhood experiences. It also provides a useful way of capturing happy events or significant achievements at a time which might otherwise be seen as stressful, traumatic or emotional.

It is emphasised that the box is there for the child and it is for the parent to think about what is important in their lives. Should separation be necessary, then the memory box can enable the parent to feel that they have given their child something of themselves. (Under these circumstances we would make copies of all photographs, drawings, etc, for the parent(s) to keep.) We are increasingly contacted by social workers for contributions to life story work and the memory box can act as a good start.

If the family is able to return to the community, then it would be hoped that the parent would continue to gather mementos for their future together.

Families First Parenting Assessment Team, Pathway Care, May 2011

PLACEMENT PLANNING MEETING

The placement planning meeting is a key opportunity to confirm the purpose of the arrangement, explain the structure and how the assessment will work, and to agree the expectations of all parties involved. This should include the parent, the foster carer, the child's social worker, the supervising social worker, and other professionals including health visitors, leaving care workers and children's guardians. Placement planning meetings need to consider both the broad placement objectives as set out in the care plan, but also need to address the very specific day-to-day issues such as house rules, contact arrangements and other practical arrangements. It is these day-to-day issues which, if not clearly agreed at the outset, can cause difficulties for both parents and foster carers and can ultimately lead to arrangements breaking down. A contract between the fostering service and parent should be drawn up and signed and dates for reviews should be set.

Adams and Bevan (2011, p. 35) cite a foster carer talking about the importance of a good placement agreement in contributing to a successful placement:

> It's useful to have the placement agreement [meeting] as early on in the placement as possible, so it's very clear what is expected and to hear what the young person expects, it helps them to settle because they know what the rules are...it's helpful for everyone.

Roles and responsibilities

It is absolutely crucial that the roles and responsibilities of the parent, foster carer and various professionals are clearly set out and agreed prior to the start of any arrangement. For professionals, this will need to include clarity about frequency and purpose of visits, and how each person will be contributing to the agreed care plan. Crucially, it is important to be clear about how any assessment will be undertaken, who will be leading on this, how it will happen, and who will contribute to this. In some settings it will be the child's social worker who leads on this assessment; in other settings the supervising social worker will undertake this work; and in still others it will be an assessor who is independent of both the child and the foster carer (see Chapter 7).

Record keeping is another important area, and the foster carer needs to know what records they are expected to keep, and how these will be shared with the parent. Adams and Bevan (2011, p. 35) cite a foster carer describing a situation where failure to do this effectively caused problems:

When they went to court I found that incredibly difficult, I thought, am I going to be at risk when she comes back, as they [the local authority] took all my notes...I don't think the mother was clear that I was recording.

Record keeping is discussed further in Chapter 7.

Child care and babysitting

As discussed earlier in this practice guide, parent and child arrangements can have different objectives and these will determine some of the issues in the placement plan.

There will be a fundamental question about who is responsible for the child: who will be undertaking the day-to-day care, feeding, comforting, getting up at night, taking responsibility for meeting health needs, arranging appointments with the health visitor or other professionals, and the like. Where there have been child protection concerns, it may be that the foster carer has a role in monitoring some of these areas, but it is essential that everyone understands what is expected of them and others.

Central to any plan will be the issue of whether the parent is in employment or education, and if so, who is responsible for the child during these periods. Even if the parent has no employment or education commitments, there is still the question of babysitting – does the carer have a responsibility to provide this and if so, how often is appropriate? A balance must be achieved between supporting the parent to succeed, without setting up an unrealistic level of support that will not be available if the parent returns to the community with their child. Some fostering services routinely offer that foster carers will babysit once a week, and ensure that this is written into the placement plan. There will also need to be clarity about caring for the child after any nights out. What time should parents be expected back, and are they then expected to take on the care of the child at that point, with the implications this has around alcohol consumption? All of these matters need to be clearly agreed in advance, and not when problems have already emerged.

House rules

Parent and child arrangements are unique in that foster carers have other adults effectively living in their home as if "placed". Sharing living space can be challenging for any unrelated adults, but this is particularly so in circumstances involving either a new parent, or an assessment of parenting involving social workers and the courts. To minimise these difficulties, it is necessary to try and manage potential areas of conflict, some of them very practical, such as where people smoke, how bathroom time is shared, and how all parties achieve some privacy and time for themselves.

Smoking

Smoking can be an issue that creates particular problems. Protecting babies from exposure to direct smoke is an important health issue (Mather and Lehner, 2007). Some people view smoking as an addiction that needs to be fed; while for others it is an unpleasant habit that impacts adversely on other people as well as the smoker. Many people, including foster carers, are not willing to let other adults smoke in their homes. The issue can be further complicated in a foster home where it will usually be expected that either the household is non-smoking, or that any smoking is undertaken away from children with arrangements in place to ensure appropriate supervision of children while this takes place. This contrasts starkly with what is deemed acceptable – if undesirable – in the community, where parents are entitled to smoke as they wish, with no regard for the impact on any children they are caring for. The expectations about children in foster homes are very different from expectations in the community, and so rules and agreements about this need to be clearly set out for parent and child fostering arrangements. This might include some compromise and flexibility, so that if birth parents smoke then they do so outside, but this might mean foster carers being willing to supervise the child while this happens. This will need to be agreed on a case by case basis, but should not be neglected in the planning stage, or it is likely to emerge as a problem at a later date.

Contact and visitors

Another area for potential conflict in parent and child arrangements is the matter of contact. This could relate to the parent's partner if he or she is not living in the foster home, or could be in relation to other family members. If the parent is also a child, then they may have a contact plan including family or friends, and this will have implications for the arrangement and indirectly, the role of the foster carer. Where the parent is an adult, it may be that their network of family and friends is not appropriate to visit the foster home, particularly where there are issues of domestic violence or substance misuse, and where this is the case, it is particularly important that arrangements are clearly set out in the plan.

Consideration should be given to the timing and impact of contact on the success of the arrangement, for example, where an assessment is working well parents are often able to make significant changes in themselves because they are protected from external influences and pressures during this process of change. The test towards the end of an arrangement is then whether they are strong enough to sustain those changes. If the partner needs to have high levels of contact and the parents are intending to be together after the arrangement, then another option to be considered would be whether both parents should be part of the arrangement and assessed together.

Consideration should also be given to the appropriateness of using a foster carer to supervise contact due to the potential conflict in interest for both carer and parent.

Agreements about contact need to include all forms of contact including phone or internet contact as an area of tension can arise where the time spent on the phone or online is impacting adversely on the care of the baby. However, this needs to be balanced against the recognition that for most people there is a wish to have contact with wider family and friends just after having a baby.

Finance and equipment

Placement agreements for parent and child arrangements will need to look at expectations around responsibility for purchasing items such as nappies, baby milk and clothes, as well as the costs of food and clothing for the parents, the latter being determined by the age and legal status of the parent, amongst other things. It is important to be clear that there is appropriate equipment available to the parent, such as pushchairs and stair gates, and if there is not, then who is responsible for purchasing these. There may also be costs such as medicines and travel to clinics that should be considered. The foster carer needs to be clear about what will be paid for out of their fostering allowance, and the parent will need to understand her or his responsibilities in order to budget accordingly. An advantage to the parent having their own budget is that they can retain their independence and responsibility for providing everything for their child. Many of the parents are care leavers and to have a carer "give them money" will reinforce their dependent status.

Arrangements for assessment

Where an arrangement is for the purposes of assessment, it is essential to be clear about what this means and how it will be undertaken, and this is discussed in depth in the following chapter. It is worth emphasising, however, that the assessment will likely only go well if these other matters – including very practical issues – are clear and agreed at the outset.

A written contract

The outcome of such a meeting needs to be contained within a written record – effectively a written contract – that sets out very clearly what has been agreed, is provided to all participants, and can be referred to subsequently when reviewing progress, or if disagreements arise. For one foster carer in the Adams and Bevan study (2011, p. 58), this was very useful:

> I could say to her, 'You go and look at your contract'...[it covered] what her role was and what mine was and when the father could visit...[and] when I'd look after the baby for her.

In Brighton and Hove, the fostering service has been making parent and child arrangements for some years, and in response to emerging experience including foster carer feedback, Donnelly and Wright (2009, p. 4) have devised a "Set-up meeting template" that covers important issues (see Appendix 9). East Sussex also has experience in this area, and has produced a very useful document that sets out in detail the things that need to be considered when making an arrangement (Appendix 10). TACT has developed a useful placement agreement format (Appendix 11), Pathway Care has drawn up a placement contract (Appendix 12) and West Sussex very helpfully sets out what is expected of parents in their parent and baby foster care practice guidance (see Box 22).

COMPLAINTS

Prior to the arrangement starting, it is essential that parents are made aware of the complaints system, and how they can address matters that they are unhappy with. It is obviously best if difficulties can be sorted out at the earliest possible stage and without resort to a formal procedure, but in some cases this will be inevitable, and right. Parents are clearly the least powerful people in this process and they need to be aware that there are independent arrangements in place to consider matters if they feel they are being treated unfairly, or if individuals are behaving in an unacceptable way. By discussing these matters at the outset, this sets out a clear framework for resolving difficulties (including informal arrangements), and this information should also be provided to parents in writing, with any other information they are given about the foster home.

BOX 22 **WEST SUSSEX COUNTY COUNCIL – EXPECTATIONS OF PARENTS**

- Parent will be expected to care for their baby/child at all times (getting baby up, bathing, feeding, changing under supervision from carer until it is agreed it is no longer necessary).
- Parent will be expected to manage the day/bedtime routine, which fits in with the foster carer's household. When parent is settling baby for bedtime routine, it is parent's responsibility to check on the child throughout the evening until they retire to bed.
- Parent will be expected to demonstrate their competence in attending to all their baby's needs and interact positively with their baby.
- Parent will be expected to shop/budget/cook for self and baby/child and attend to all clothes washing and ironing. Parent will keep his/her room tidy and leave kitchen/bathroom in a tidy/clean condition after use.
- Personal clothing and belongings must be kept in parent's own room. The foster carer cannot be responsible for property or articles that are lost or damaged.
- Parents will contribute to the wellbeing of everyone in the foster carer's home and in public by demonstrating non-aggressive/non-threatening behaviours.
- If agreed in the contract, the foster carer will offer babysitting one evening per week; parent will provide 24-hour notice for request.
- Foster carer may make random room checks to ensure safety of parent and child and therefore all bedroom doors must be kept unlocked.
- The foster carer will write accurate daily record sheets, which will be shared daily with parent and signed by both parent and carer. If there are any differences of opinion these should be discussed and recorded.
- The foster carer will complete and share the safe caring plan with the parent.
- Smoking is not permitted inside the foster carer's home. No alcohol to be consumed or kept in carer's home.
- No involvement with any illegal substances is permitted in the foster carer's home. However, it is recognised that some parents may be supported in a parent and baby placement when parent is supervised by a treatment programme.
- Parent to inform carer and child's social worker of any appointments/assessments, etc, and check if childcare cover is approved.
- Parent's circumstances/history is strictly confidential to the named foster carer.

Extract from West Sussex County Council Parent and Baby Foster Care Practice Guidance, 2010

MATCHING

Matching can only be effective when the purpose of the arrangement is clearly identified along with the needs of the parent and child. When undertaken well, the matching process will set out needs of the parent and child, and identify a foster carer who is well placed to meet these. This should take into consideration the following factors:

- availability of suitably approved carers and when the arrangement is required;

- geography of foster home including proximity to parent's support networks and transport links;

- size and nature of the accommodation in relation to the identified needs;

- objective of the arrangement (support or assessment);

- any medical needs of the parent or child, and the carer's ability to meet these;

- the parent's motivation and how the carer might work with this;

- other household members including children;

- known history of the parent being considered;

- language and cultural needs and the carer's ability to meet these;

- the "chemistry" between parent and carer (where known);

- any issues arising out of the risk assessment.

A key consideration must always be around the issues of language, ethnicity, religion (including ensuring opportunities for the child's religious observance) and culture. It will be important for parents and foster carers to communicate effectively with each other, and if they do not speak the same language, this sets up a potential barrier from the outset. Furthermore, different cultures will often have different attitudes and perspectives, and what is acceptable in one culture might well be viewed as problematic in another. These fostering arrangements ask two families to live together in a single household, and very different attitudes to things like appropriate modesty and permitted foodstuffs can create difficulties, particularly in a relationship that already has potential tensions built into it. This does not mean that it is always necessary to match exactly for ethnicity and culture (if that is even possible), but it does mean that these issues need to be taken into account when looking to match. It is generally accepted that some foster carers have a better understanding of equality and diversity issues than others, and if some parents are openly racist then this also needs to be considered, as foster carers should not be expected to tolerate overt racism in their homes.

Efforts should also be made to take into account the wishes and feelings of the parent, and this will need to account for issues such as whether a female parent feels comfortable living with unrelated men in the household, whether they want other children around, the locality they want to live in, and how they feel about any pets that the foster carer may have.

There are also aspects of matching that are hard to define on paper, and if it is possible for parents to meet with proposed foster carers before agreeing a match then this can be very helpful in looking at whether the "chemistry" is right. Adams and Bevan (2011) suggest that where parents want to be in the foster home and "fit in", this can contribute to a successful outcome, and they note the potential benefits of parents getting to know foster carers before they move in where that is possible. Foster carers in Donnelly and Wright's study (2009, p. 4) made the same point. It must be accepted that the nature of child care social work means that such pre-arrangement activity is not always possible, but nevertheless it should be considered where it can be achieved.

PLANNING FOR ENDINGS

Right from the start it is helpful to think about the potential ending of the arrangement or "exit plans". This will involve being clear with parents about what circumstances might necessitate an arrangement being terminated: this might include a parent refusing to engage in the assessment, or failing to adhere to specific contact plans, or providing details of the foster home to a partner or other with a history of violence. If a parent needs to leave the arrangement prior to completion of an assessment or other planned work, what will this mean for the child? It is necessary to be clear whether another parent and child arrangement will be offered; whether the parent can leave with the child (unlikely unless a risk assessment has concluded this is appropriate); whether there is an appropriate family member available to take the child; whether the child will remain with the parent and child foster carer; or whether that child will move to another foster carer without the parent. It is not helpful to try to resolve these questions in the midst of a breakdown of the arrangement, and so this needs to be clearly established at the outset.

If the ending is more positive, with the parent being deemed suitable to care for their child in the community, then the planning will be different, but equally as important (Donnelly and Wright, 2009, p. 6). It will be necessary to ensure that the parent has appropriate accommodation to move to with the equipment that they might need for caring for the child and that there is an appropriate support structure in place for both parent and child. In some circumstances semi-independent living might be appropriate. While the scenario of a positive ending provides scope for planning to take place as the arrangement progresses, it is important that the ending is considered at the outset and at every stage throughout the arrangement. Both Somerset and West Sussex County Councils forged effective links with housing managers in their area, and carefully considered support required at the end of the arrangement in moving parents and children into the community (see Box 23).

Pathway Care holds "placement ending meetings" which are usually planned for a couple of weeks after the parent has left. These provide an opportunity for carers and staff to reflect on the arrangement, to gather statistical information, and to identify any training needs of carers and their availability for the next arrangement. A "placement ending meetings" form from Pathway Care is included as Appendix 13.

BOX 23

WEST SUSSEX COUNTY COUNCIL – GOOD PRACTICE EXAMPLE FOR MOVING PLACEMENTS ON

In West Sussex the family placement social worker initially contacted and visited one of the housing managers to discuss ways of working together for the small group of successful parent and baby placements who require accommodation, and was invited to a meeting of housing managers for the whole of West Sussex.

This gave the social worker an opportunity to explain her role, how parent and baby placements are used, statistics, and the difficulties faced by parents following placements ending. The managers agreed to be her links to discuss individual cases at the beginning of each placement, and to consider the housing options, including an independent living scheme for looked after parents.

The meeting provided the social worker with a greater understanding of the housing "band" system that West Sussex uses and she was able to negotiate some priority for parents in certain circumstances. These links with the housing managers have also enabled her to gain knowledge of other available options for parents if the local housing associations are not able to help, such as the rent deposit scheme in the private housing sector.

Alongside this, West Sussex has developed a post-placement support programme that follows a successful parent and baby placement. It is usually negotiated at the placement planning meeting and considered within the regular reviews. This outreach programme enables the foster carer to support the parent and baby back into the community in a gradual and planned way, and, once the outreach programme finishes, the parent is hopefully set up with supports via other providers and professionals.

Information provided by West Sussex County Council, February 2011

7

Assessing parents and good enough parenting

One of the unique features of parent and child fostering is that foster carers are usually not solely or even primarily responsible for the direct care of children, but contribute to either supporting or assessing birth parents in their care of the child. This chapter focuses specifically on arrangements that have been set up for the purpose of assessment, usually in the context of potential or active court proceedings.

MODELS OF ASSESSMENT

There are three basic models for undertaking parenting assessments in the context of parent and child arrangements.

a)   Team-based assessor

In this model, there is a social work assessor within the parent and child team whose key role is to undertake assessments and present these in court. Commissioners will be purchasing or accessing a package that consists of both the parent and child arrangement and a social work assessment that will be undertaken while the parent and child live with the carer. The strengths of this model will lie in the expertise of the team and the coherence of approach that will come from familiarity with particular ways of working including agreed roles and responsibilities, and established working relationships across the team. An assessment format will be used that is structured and tested, and the assessor will be well placed to service court requirements, being able to demonstrate clearly from the outset how an assessment will be progressed.

Some local authorities additionally, where the resources are available, involve the parent in attending a parenting assessment programme at a family or children's centre.

b) Child's social worker as assessor

With this model, the fostering service offers a parent and child arrangement and supports that foster carer in the same way that they would with any other mainstream placement. Here, the remit of the fostering service is distinctly in relation to the foster carer, and the supervising social worker has a limited remit in terms of assessing the parent by working closely with the foster carer to ensure that information and observations are passed onto the primary assessor. The assessment task will fall to the child's social worker in the same way that it would if the parent and child were living in their own accommodation, or if the child was in foster care and the parent in the community. This model has the advantage of allowing continuity in the relationship between social worker and parent, but in a court context may not be accepted as an impartial assessment, and may necessitate commissioning independent assessments. Furthermore, there is the risk that the assessment relies on observation and is reactive, rather than being based on an established and recognised structure.

c) Independent assessor

Local authorities may choose to commission an independent social worker to undertake this assessment but that might not achieve the other benefits associated with clarity of roles, processes, and structure that can be achieved within an established team approach.

THE ROLE OF THE FOSTER CARERS IN ASSESSMENT

There is a general consensus among most fostering services that while foster carers should be a significant contributor to assessments – they have been described as the "eyes and ears" for the assessing social worker – for the most part it is not desirable that they lead this process. There is the issue of skill base – the skills required for a social work assessment are very different from those required for fostering. It can be difficult for a person to be objective and avoid value judgements when they have formed a relationship with someone they are living with. This can potentially result in feelings of antagonism and anger, or conversely, affection and empathy, neither of which is helpful in completing a fair and impartial parenting assessment. There will always be exceptions to this, but someone with social work assessment skills, who wants to foster, and who can maintain professional objectivity in the context of sharing a home with someone, will be a rare person. That said, foster carers can and must play a significant part within any good parent and child fostering assessment, and in some cases courts have been keen to clarify exactly what the foster carer's role and responsibility will be prior to the arrangement being made.

BOX 24   **SOUTHAMPTON CITY COUNCIL**

In Southampton a foster carer from the Parent & Child Scheme took on a specific piece of work supervising contact and observing the parents' care of the child over a 12-week period. The arrangements for this were recorded in a Commissioning Statement which was filed with the court during care proceedings setting out the role of the carer and the Parent and Child Co-ordinator. There was clarity that the foster carer was not responsible for the final decision about the child's care but that her evidence would be submitted to the local authority for them to consider in their planning for the child.

PRE-ARRANGEMENT ASSESSMENT AND PLANNING

In any parenting assessment, it is necessary to be clear about the aims of the assessment, and also to be clear about what might come out of it for each of the parties. Pathway Care helpfully sets out its aims in exactly these terms (see Box 25 below).

In order to give a parent the maximum chance of successfully completing an assessment and continuing to parent their child, it is necessary to undertake a full and detailed assessment of their personal and individual circumstances prior to their living in the foster home. In part, this is discussed in the previous chapter, but this did not focus specifically on the assessment aspect. A good pre-arrangement assessment needs to set out the concerns about the parenting; be clear about the identified risks; and identify what behaviours need to be evidenced, or change, in order that professionals will be less concerned. There will also be a need to look at the specific vulnerabilities that a person brings, as well as considering their strengths.

This means that questions that were previously considered in terms of a risk assessment, or suitability for parent and child fostering, also need to be considered specifically in terms of their relevance to assessment. This might include practical aspects such as substance misuse or inappropriate relationships, but could also include consideration of the parent's own childhood and how this might impact on their parenting. It might include consideration of a person's age and maturity, and how this will impact on developing an appropriate relationship with their child. Only by considering these various aspects on an individual basis will it be possible to ensure an entirely fair and objective assessment process.

BOX 25   **PATHWAY CARE – THE AIMS OF PARENT AND CHILD ASSESSMENTS**

To provide local authorities and courts with:

- a final report that addresses the issues identified in the Assessment Framework
- evidence to make decisions in respect of the child's welfare
- information to create viable and realistic care plans
- recommendations in respect of any support the family may need to sustain long-term success
- expertise that will withstand examination both in and out of court

To provide parents with:

- a proper opportunity to demonstrate that they care for their child(ren) which is fair and takes into consideration the family's particular needs
- constructive guidance and teaching to assist them in identifying and then meeting their goals
- an opportunity to observe good parenting as modelled by the carers

To ensure the assessment process is:

- planned and structured
- transparent, fair and evidence based

Adapted from Families First Parenting Assessment brochure, Pathway Care, 2010.

EQUALITIES AND MULTI-DISCIPLINARY WORKING

In planning the assessment, it is also crucial that consideration is given to issues of equality and diversity, and that will mean taking account of issues including ethnicity, culture, class, and disability, amongst others. There are significant cultural differences in how different groups parent children, and it is essential that these are fully accounted for when judgements are reached about a person's parenting abilities.

There are also particular issues that need to be considered in relation to disability, including learning difficulty, and these need full and expert consideration at the outset. For example, there are likely to be significant benefits from undertaking a cognitive assessment of parents with learning difficulties, in order to think about how they learn best, and so to be able to tailor an assessment or programme accordingly.

Carers need to have had some specific input on working with parents with learning difficulties and be aware of and understand the findings of any cognitive assessments that have been undertaken on the parent.

It will also be necessary to ensure that carers have an understanding of the needs of disabled children, including the additional demands this may make on a parent caring for them.

BOX 26	**HEALTH ISSUES IN THE GREENAWAY STUDY**

In Greenway's study (2010), there was a case where the child had health needs and the carer was seen as having a support role. The carer had visited the parent and child in hospital daily for six days before they moved into the foster home and the carer had had experience of one of her own children having similar difficulties and felt this created a bond between them. The parent's view of the arrangement was that 'it would give me a few weeks to learn how to look after (the child), obviously with his needs, give me a chance to learn to look after him'. When asked if there had been anything that was particularly positive or difficult as the placement went on, the parent said that the fact that she had learnt to insert a G-tube (for the child's additional health needs) was particularly positive. The placement was apparently successful as the parent gradually began to spend more time in the community and eventually took the child home.

In such cases, a good assessment will need to involve professionals from disciplines other than children's social work, and will likely include community paediatric, midwifery and health visiting services, but could also include psychology, disability, and substance misuse services. Pathway Care provided a good example of effective multi-disciplinary working (see Box 27).

BOX 27   **PATHWAY CARE – A CASE STUDY IN MULTI-DISCIPLINARY WORKING**

Emma was first introduced to Pathway Care just before she gave birth to her baby, George. Her significant learning disability, unstable mental health, childhood abuse, tendency to form relationships with violent men, social isolation and unreliable and fluctuating relationship with her mother had all combined to prevent her from looking after her oldest daughter who had been placed within the extended family. Prior to placement, George's social worker, Emma's occupational therapist and her speech and language therapist met with us, as the fostering provider, and with the foster carer. This enabled us to have a full understanding of Emma and the best ways of communicating with her, and we were also able to explain how we undertook an assessment, enabling Emma's team to reassure her before she moved in.

The assessment in relation to George proved to be exceptionally difficult, with the foster carer needing to be extremely vigilant to safeguard George while also coping with Emma's unpredictability.

It was only possible to manage this because of the good communication between the provider and referrer, and due to the ongoing contribution of the various adult services. As Emma's mental health deteriorated, an adult psychiatrist became involved, and fortunately he was willing to offer flexible support and consultation either by telephone or by home visit, and this was invaluable.

It was initially anticipated that Emma would be unable to manage more than a few weeks of being in placement, but due to the time and care put into introductions and planning, combined with sustained high quality communication between the various professionals and services, Emma stayed in the placement for seven months.

Families First Parenting Assessment Team, Pathway Care, 2011

ASSESSMENT STRUCTURE AND CONTENT

Whichever model is used, it is necessary to have clarity about the structure of the assessment: what will it entail, who will be involved, how long will it take, what is expected of the parents, and what will be expected of all the professionals involved. Some fostering services have a very clearly defined 12-week assessment that includes one or two reviews and weekly progress meetings; others will set out arrangements on a more individual basis, depending on court dates and individual circumstances. Whatever is decided, it needs to be clearly set out in writing as an agreement or contract, and this will be the document to refer to in the event of disagreements or difficulties.

It is also crucial to be clear about what is going to be covered in an assessment, and some fostering services use the Assessment of Children in Need Framework headings, but others have devised their own specific criteria (see Box 28).

BOX 28   **SOMERSET COUNTY COUNCIL – ASSESSMENT CRITERIA TO ADDRESS SPECIFIC AREAS OF RISK**

- Mother's ability to consistently meet child's basic day-to-day needs and provide him with safe care

- Mother's ability to prioritise child's needs above that of her own

- Mother's ability to recognise and understand the risks to child from domestic violence and her ability to protect him from such a risk

- Mother's view of her relationship and separation from partner

- Mother's ability to co-operate and work with professionals, and take on board and implement advice given in short, medium and long term

(Template taken from Perry D, Bath and North East Somerset Community Based Parenting Assessment Project, 2009)

RECORD KEEPING

Whatever the specific assessment model used, foster carer records will need to contribute to this and may be used by the assessor as evidence in drafting court reports. Fostering services give examples of foster carers' records being appended to social work court statements, and note that foster carers are often required to make statements regarding their records, and attend court to give evidence and be cross-examined about them. It is therefore essential that foster carers are trained and supported to keep good written records, and feel able to justify them as accurate and appropriate.

With this in mind, fostering services need to provide an appropriate format for foster carers' record keeping, and need to ensure that their policies promote an open and transparent approach. Best practice might involve foster carers sharing their records with birth parents on a regular basis, allowing the parent to agree or disagree with the accuracy, record any disagreements or make any comments in relation to what has been written.

It should be remembered that, in addition to being used as evidence in courts, records can be used as a tool to help parents see where they are making progress and have a written record of that as "proof" in discussions with social workers or to be included in their representations to court. They can also be used to help a parent understand where they are falling short, and can be helpful in contributing to improvements where the parent can reflect on what is being written, and make changes. Even where the parent might be unable to make the necessary changes, it is beneficial to help them understand why their child is being removed if that is the outcome, and to feel that they have been given every opportunity to address concerns. At times, this might mean they are able to recognise that they are unable to meet their child's needs, and participate positively in making alternative plans.

There are different structures for record keeping, but carers could be expected to keep daily records, weekly or monthly summaries, and reports provided at the end of the arrangement. Daily records tend to use a chronological or events-based approach that describes what happened during the day, and that was relevant to the child, and what that says about parenting capacity (see examples of West Sussex and Kasper Fostering in Appendices 14 and 15).

Weekly summaries and reports at the end of the arrangement need a more structured approach, and a clear framework for recording that allows carers to set out themes and developments over that period. The Assessment Framework can be useful in this and carers can focus on any specific areas that have been highlighted as particularly relevant for that individual parent and their child, but some fostering services have preferred to devise their own formats for this purpose. Various fostering services have developed a very useful weekly summary format (see Appendices 17 and 18). In any record keeping it is essential that the foster carer records facts and observations in appropriate detail, and where opinions and reflections are included, they are identified as such.

A STRUCTURED APPROACH

This practice guide cannot cover in any depth the issues involved in undertaking effective assessments of parents and their children, as this is a huge topic better covered elsewhere. However, it is important that where fostering services or others are making assessments, they do this from a position of competence and knowledge, using a structured approach, and making use of appropriate resources and tools. A number of fostering services use the Department of Health (2000) Assessment Framework with the associated tools. Other resources include the City of Salford Community and Social Services (2000) *Conducting Family Assessments: A practice guide* (further information is available on the publisher's website www.russellhouse.co.uk) and McGraw *et al* (1998)

Parent Assessment Manual Programme (further information is available on the publisher website at www.pamsweb.co.uk/index.html).

Some fostering services have developed innovative ways of assessing parents with learning difficulties or offering support with developing language and play skills. For examples of these, see Pathway Care's use of "widgets" outlined in Box 29 and ISP Rainham's Talk and Play group in Box 30.

BOX 29   PATHWAY CARE – USE OF "WIDGETS"

Pathway Care uses widgets with parents who have learning difficulties or with those who simply find it difficult to keep to routines or remember things. Widgets provide a visual prompt to support parents in completing tasks which they might otherwise forget. Pathway Care has used them for reminding parents about a range of tasks including taking medication, changing nappies, doing the laundry, paying bills and keeping appointments. The widget system encourages the parent to start taking responsibility for, and control over, their own lives.

The content of the widget system is decided together with the parent, with the parent identifying where they need help. The parent helps to make the widgets – either by writing the task down or finding pictures if this is easier for them to understand. For example, one mother found a picture of a bin and a nappy a better prompt than a card stating 'Put nappies in the bin'. The cards are then laminated and backed with Velcro and attached to a board.

At the beginning of each day the parent decides which tasks need to be completed that day and the relevant widgets are put on the board. The parent refers to the board throughout the day, taking the widgets off or moving them to a different area on the board as tasks are completed.

L had significant learning difficulties and became easily overwhelmed by the tasks she had to complete each day. She had very low self-esteem and no self-confidence, both of which were boosted by her taking responsibility for what needed to be done and being able to rely on widgets (i.e. herself) rather than on other people. L returned home and has continued to use widgets in the community.

Families First Parenting Assessment Team, Pathway Care, 2011

BOX 30   **ISP RAINHAM – TALK AND PLAY GROUP**

At ISP Rainham, staff have found that, given the adverse circumstances that the parents find themselves in, it is often difficult to persuade them to attend local groups alongside their children. As the parents and children have often been placed outside of their immediate home area, they are reluctant to join groups and access services as they either do not know anyone else or do not know what these groups are like as they have not attended them in the past.

To aid the parent's participation and to increase their parenting skills, ISP Rainham has introduced a Talk and Play group. These sessions are for parents and children in placement together to meet other families in a fun and relaxed group. The group is designed to help develop early play and language skills and encourages parents to notice the positive effects their interactions have. It also provides opportunities for parents to share experiences of parenthood.

The group is facilitated by an ISP speech and language therapist and an assistant speech and language therapist. The group is held every other week.

The group has had good participation and parents who have been attending but are now due to leave placement have been asking to continue coming. ISP Rainham has agreed to allow this to continue in the short term at no additional cost to either the local authority or the parent. The hope is that the parent's confidence is increased further allowing them to access and participate in groups that are being run within their communities.

There have been some difficulties within the group such as parents seeing the group as a useful childminding resource whilst they go to the local shops, parents making comparisons between their own situations and then wanting the same arrangement that other parents may have. Building trust with parents can be difficult especially during the first few sessions. Where there are two parents together it becomes more difficult to get them to engage within the group and they will often sit throughout in their own self-contained unit. The group continues to grow but perhaps the greatest challenge is being able to manage an ever-changing group often with new members and keeping the sessions focused on the parent's interactions with their child.

ISP Rainham are continuing to develop the service and have had positive feedback from the parents who attend, foster parents and LA social workers. Many of the foster parents report a greater willingness of the parent(s) to interact with their child in a more positive way and make more time for communication. In the near future there are plans for an agency psychotherapist to observe the group and provide feedback on how the interactions between everyone involved are helping the parents and children develop their skills. As a further extension of the group, there is also a possibility of offering video interaction guidance through the onsite educational psychologist to parents to help them identify and build on the positive interactions they have developed.

ISP Rainham, January 2010

GOOD ENOUGH PARENTING

It is generally recognised that "good enough" parenting is hard to define, but in broad terms the concept has been useful in distinguishing between the notion of perfect parenting and inevitable mistakes, errors of judgement and lapses that are a part of all parenting and being parented. With this, there is still an enormous spectrum of parenting approaches, and establishing criteria that mark out those that fall within the legal definition of "significant harm" is challenging. There are helpful approaches to this (Hindley *et al*, 2006) but there is little doubt that it requires considerable knowledge and experience of child development and parenting to understand this well.

With parent and child arrangements, these issues are particularly significant. The foster carer's experience and views about "good enough" parenting may clash with the parents' views, and by the very nature of the arrangement, it is likely that the parent's approach to or the circumstances of their parenting are not good enough.

This is hugely significant, and brings an entirely different dimension to the practice of fostering. For some foster carers, who came into fostering because of their desire to provide very high quality care to vulnerable and disadvantaged children, this can create a situation that they are unable to accept.

Parent and child carers do need to work with this, and learn to make judgements about what is good enough, and what is not. It is very hard to set clear guidelines about what this means in practice, as circumstances will vary in each case. However, it is clear that foster carers need to be trained and supported to know when to intervene because a child is at risk, and be fully aware of their responsibilities in relation to child protection matters. They must also be able to make judgements about when it is helpful to intervene in an effort to improve parenting capacity, and when to step back and allow parents some autonomy, even where their parenting style might create problems, or might clash with the carer's views about this. At times, it may be that the best way to intervene is through quietly role-modelling a different approach, and talking to the parent about this at a later more appropriate time. All of these are difficult judgements, and need to be considered on an ongoing basis in the context of a reflective supervisory relationship.

MANAGING RISK

In all parent and child arrangements involving an assessment of parenting, there is, by definition, a level of risk involved, and the parent would not be subject to assessment if this was not the case. Risk assessment has been considered in a previous chapter, in the context of planning for the arrangement, and the fact is that risk needs to be considered on an ongoing basis, not just at the beginning of the arrangement. It is crucial that this is very clearly acknowledged, and that foster carers are empowered and supported to monitor and assess that risk, and to take action in circumstances when it becomes too great to accept. This support will include specific training about risk management, and discussions in the assessment phase about what this might entail, and whether the potential foster carer will feel able to undertake this aspect of the role. It will also involve regular face to face meetings with their supervising social worker or other social work professional, and good practice requires specific consideration of risk on each occasion. Risk assessment must be an ongoing activity that is informed by close observation, reflection, and clear responsibility for action where necessary.

It is also important that the matter is covered openly and honestly at the Placement Planning Meeting, and that the specific details around monitoring are considered. For example, is it appropriate for the foster carer to enter the parent's bedroom if they do not respond to a knock on the door? If the baby is crying at night and the parent is slow to respond, how is the carer expected to deal with this? Is it appropriate in any circumstances for the foster carer to have a baby monitor in the parent's room, or does that breach the privacy of the parent? Furthermore, does the need to do this suggest that the risk is just too high to be managed in a foster home? There are probably no right or wrong answers to these general questions, but they are the sort of thing that needs to be clearly agreed at the outset, and foster carers need to feel confident about their role in relation to them.

8
Policies and procedures

As has been noted earlier in this guide, the importance of fostering services having clear and specific policies and procedures on the management of parent and child arrangements has been highlighted in statutory guidance, research studies and two serious case reviews involving parent and child arrangements.

For fostering services where such arrangements happen infrequently, these may need to be included with or appended to other fostering policy documents, but for those fostering providers offering specific schemes or parent and child services, it is important that comprehensive policies and procedures are in place to ensure that commissioners of the service and all individuals involved in the arrangement have a shared understanding of what is being offered and their roles and responsibilities and the expectations of them.

The following suggested list of areas to be covered by the fostering service's policies and procedures is drawn from the issues which have been more fully explored in this practice guide.

- [ ] A Statement of Purpose/aims and objectives of parent and child arrangements and the context and requirements for specific schemes.

- [ ] Recruitment and assessment criteria, including skills and experience required by parent and child carers and provision of training and support.

- [ ] The legal context of parent and child arrangements, including both childcare and fostering legislation in the relevant countries and the implications for the status of both parents and children.

- [ ] The referral process, which should include what written information is required about the background circumstances of the case and what the parent and child arrangement is expected to provide before an arrangement can be made.

- [ ] Matching procedures and how carers will be selected to include geographical considerations, taking account of any existing placements or birth children and support needs.

- [ ] Pre-arrangement planning process including pre-birth assessments, risk assessments, planning meetings and reviews and the roles and responsibilities of the childcare social worker and supervising social worker.

☐ Assessment process, highlighting differences between assessment and support arrangements, expectations of record keeping, assessment and court reports and the roles and responsibilities of social workers and foster carers in the assessment.

☐ Safer caring to include undertaking risk assessments before and where needed during arrangements, expectations of the parent within the foster home, e.g. smoking or babysitting arrangements.

☐ Child protection issues within the context of the fostering service's main child protection policy but focusing on specific issues relating to parent and child arrangements, e.g. access to out of hours support for the foster carer, reporting issues of concern re: parenting and managing risks to a child and responses where a parent does not return to the foster home when expected.

☐ Financial arrangements to include payments for carers, tax and insurance issues for foster carers and financial issues relating to parents, e.g. claiming relevant benefits and agreeing their areas of responsibility in providing for the child.

☐ Planning for the move from the foster home, to include liaison with other departments, e.g. housing, provision of aftercare support by the foster carer, and planning for children where the outcome of the parent and child arrangement results in separation of the parent and child.

In addition to drawing up policies and procedures, fostering services are also developing forms to go alongside these to be used at the various stages of referral, planning and review and tools for assessment and recording to be used by social workers and foster carers to contribute to the assessment report. Some examples of these from various fostering services have been included in the appendices for reference.

Conclusion

It has become clear over the last few years that parent and child fostering is a growing area of provision and there are now a number of independent fostering agencies and local authorities that are investing in specific schemes whilst others are continuing to make parent and child arrangements in response to individual cases.

As has been highlighted earlier, there is little conclusive research evidence at this time for the success of these arrangements or comparisons of outcomes with other types of community-based or residential provision and it is to be hoped that this will be forthcoming in the future to inform the development of these services.

During the time of writing this guide, there has been some statutory guidance issued in England by the Department for Education (Volume 4, Annex B) which has started to answer some of the dilemmas posed by arrangements which sometimes do not fit within existing regulations. However, there is still a need for further clarification about how these arrangements can be managed within existing legislation and whether there is a need for further regulation and/or guidance.

In the absence of such regulation and guidance, there are only a small proportion of parent and children arrangements that fall under the remit of OFSTED and the equivalent regulatory bodies, which is of concern given the complex nature of such arrangements. This means that at present we have to look to the emerging good practice being developed within the statutory and independent sectors to try to ensure that some consistency can be achieved – this was very much the intention of this guide.

Foster carers are having to develop new skills and knowledge, so training and support are essential to assist them in adjusting to new expectations and responsibilities and it is important that fostering services look creatively at how these can be offered. This is not an area of work where an arrangement should be considered outside the foster carer's terms of approval unless this follows a review process which identifies that the carer can demonstrate the required skills and experiences. The additional areas identified in the appendices provide clear guidance about the need for careful thought and preparation about what will be involved and the abilities of the carer to adapt to the focus of these arrangements.

It is clear that there are inherent risks in offering parent and child assessments within the context of a family home and so it is essential that services offering such arrangements have clear policies and procedures so that such risks can be minimised. Some of the dilemmas highlighted, for example, whether there should be other looked after children or birth children in the home, need to be carefully considered and reflected in these policies.

Planning before the parent and child move into the foster home is crucial in ensuring that there is sufficient time to prepare parents and carers for what is expected of them. Where this is not possible, fostering services must ensure that sufficient information is provided at the point of referral so that they are confident about the viability of the assessment arrangement. It is obvious that arrangements being requested by a social worker telephoning from court do not offer the best chance of a well matched, well planned arrangement. Where there are known risk factors, such as mental health issues, domestic violence or drug misuse, there must be a risk assessment undertaken to inform whether a family-based setting is the appropriate resource – cost of parent and child arrangements must not be the overriding factor.

It is crucial that the primary focus is on achieving permanence for the child, and for babies in particular, that there is recognition that timescales are at a premium. Social workers will need to acknowledge that even within the security of parent and child fostering arrangements, the parent may not be able to support the development of a healthy, secure attachment relationship with their baby and services need to ensure that there is regular review of the arrangement.

Where assessment is an identified aspect of the arrangement, there needs to be clarity about the roles and responsibilities of all involved and we would suggest that the foster carer, whilst making a significant contribution to the assessment, should not be given the responsibility of producing the assessment – in our view this must be a social work role.

The other area where significant planning is needed is in developing links with courts, CAFCASS and solicitors, so that best use is made of these arrangements, and making strategic links with other partner agencies to provide services such as housing where needed to achieve a successful outcome or to offer counselling and support services where there is an unplanned ending. It is to be hoped that the more this area of work receives formal recognition as a valuable option, the more opportunities are likely to be created to support the good work that is already in place.

These arrangements are pushing the boundaries of what has traditionally been seen as the role of the foster carer and also what work can be undertaken within a family home. It will be important to learn from current and future research, to share best practice and to listen to the views and experiences of foster carers and parents who have lived within a parent and child arrangement.

Local authorities and independent fostering agencies should set up systems for monitoring outcomes in parent and child arrangements, consulting with carers and gathering the views of birth parents, and use these to inform future developments in practice. It is to be hoped that the same spirit of co-operation that was shown by contributors to this publication will continue to prevail so that best practice can continue to be shared and promoted.

APPENDICES

Appendix 1
Annex B
Volume 4: Fostering services
Department for Education

ANNEX B: PARENT AND CHILD ARRANGEMENTS

Introduction

1. A local authority sometimes wishes to commission an assessment of a parent's ability to safeguard and promote the welfare of his or her child, to inform its decision making about the provision of support services or intervention through care proceedings. Sometimes the court will request such an assessment within the framework of care proceedings. Most commonly these are arrangements for mothers and their babies.

2. Residential assessments may take place in residential family centres. A residential family centre is regulated under the Care Standards Act 2000 and the Residential Family Centres Regulations 2002. They are required to register with Ofsted and are subject to inspection by Ofsted, and to meet the National Minimum Standards for Residential Family Centres published by the Department of Health.

3. Residential family centres are defined as establishments where accommodation is provided for a child and their parents, the parents' capacity to respond to the child's needs and safeguard their welfare is monitored and assessed, and parents are given such advice, guidance or counselling as is considered necessary.

4. An increasingly common alternative to assessment in a residential family centre is the arrangement whereby children and their parents live with foster carers for the purposes of assessment. A foster carer's household is not an establishment, and so cannot be regarded as a residential family centre.

5. The sections below set out the different scenarios whereby arrangements may be made for a parent (or parents) and their child (or children) to live with foster carers for the purposes of an assessment. A foster carer is a person who has undergone checks and an assessment and has been approved as a foster parent by a local authority or an independent fostering provider.

A voluntary arrangement by the local authority where the child is not looked after

6. Where a local authority wish to assess a parent's parenting capacity in the context of support provided to the child/family under section 17 of the Children Act 1989 or pre care proceedings, this would need to be with the agreement of the parent. The local authority may decide to make an arrangement with the family to live with a local authority foster carer to make the assessment, rather than to make use of a residential family centre.

7. Since in this case the child is not looked after by the local authority, none of the provisions of the Children Act 1989 relating to looked after children will apply, and the foster carer will not be acting in their capacity as a foster carer under the Fostering Services (England) Regulations 2011. In such a case the local authority will need to be satisfied that the arrangement is appropriate, in the sense that the foster carers have the necessary skills to participate in the assessment, and will not place at risk the welfare of any foster child who is placed in the household.

A voluntary placement by the local authority where the child is looked after

8. In a situation where the child is looked after and the parents are 18 or older, the provisions relating to looked after children will apply in relation to the child only. The child will be placed with the foster carer under section 22 of the Children Act 1989, and the responsible authority will be under a duty to make the most appropriate placement available for both the parent and child. In making the placement it will therefore need to consider the skills and capacity of the foster carer, notwithstanding that the assessment of the parent's ability is not covered by the 2011 Regulations.

9. Although the child will be fostered by the foster carer, the child's parent or parents will also be living with the child in the foster carer's household. As the parent will not be a looked after child, the provisions in respect of looked after children will not apply to them, regardless

of whether the parent is under 18 or is older or has previously been a looked after child.

10. In these circumstances the parent will still hold parental responsibility in respect of their child, and be living in the same household as the child's foster carer. It will therefore be vital that respective roles and arrangements for delegated authority are clarified when the arrangements are being made. These must be set out in the placement plan. The foster carer's task in relation to undertaking an assessment of the parent's capabilities will not be governed by the 2011 Regulations, but will be closely aligned with their responsibilities towards the looked after child.

11. The fostering service and the responsible authority will need to satisfy themselves that the proposed arrangements will not impact unduly on the foster carer's responsibilities towards other children. Any necessary support should be provided to enable the arrangements to succeed. As with any placement when another child is already placed with the foster carer, the responsible authority for that child would need to agree to the new arrangements.

12. For the purposes of the 2011 Regulations, a parent living with a foster carer in the above circumstances is a member of the foster carer's household. The fostering service's safeguarding policy must include a statement of measures to be taken to safeguard children placed with foster carers before any arrangements are made for a parent and child to join the household. The 2011 Regulations allow for CRB checks to be obtained but there is no requirement for these to be undertaken as a prerequisite to the individual joining the household (regulation 26 and 28(3)).

A voluntary placement by the local authority where both the child and parent are looked after

13. Where both the child and the parent are looked after the provisions relating to looked after children will apply to both. The duties in relation to section 22 of the 1989 Act, as outlined in paragraph 8, will apply in respect of the placements of both the child and the parent.

An arrangement directed by the courts where the child is looked after

14. Where care proceedings are in progress, the court may require an assessment of the child and their parents.

15. If the child is subject to an interim care order under section 38(6), and the court directs a parenting assessment but leaves it up to the local authority how that assessment is organised, the local authority may decide that the parent and child will live with a foster carer for the purpose. This will be a placement of a looked after child by the local authority and so the placement will be governed by the 2011 Regulations.

16. Even if the court directs that an assessment be made by a foster carer, the placement will still be a local authority placement and the 2011 Regulations will apply.

Placement with parents

17. Children who are in care may also be placed with their parents (or someone else who has parental responsibility for them) under regulations 15 – 20 of the 2010 Regulations. While such children are looked after children and fall within the 2010 Regulations, they do not fall within the 2011 Regulations as they are not fostered children. This includes where a child is placed with their parents and the parents and that child then live with foster carers.

The usual fostering limit

18. The usual fostering limit applies to the placement of looked after children, and so a parent who is living in a parent and child arrangement with a foster carer does not count towards that limit unless he or she is themselves a looked after child. However, the impact of the parent being within the household must be taken into account in considering the placement of any looked after children.

© Department for Education 2011

Appendix 2
Additional assessment criteria for child and parent assessment foster carers – Leeds Social Care

Additional assessment criteria for child and parent assessment foster carers in line with CWDC *Training, Support and Development Standards for Foster Care*

UNDERSTAND THE PRINCIPLES AND VALUES ESSENTIAL FOR FOSTERING CHILDREN AND YOUNG PEOPLE/UNDERSTAND YOUR ROLE AS A FOSTER CARER/UNDERSTAND THE DEVELOPMENT OF CHILDREN AND YOUNG PEOPLE

1.   **An ability to provide a good standard of care to other people's children, which promotes healthy, emotional, physical and sexual development as well as their health and educational achievement**

- What do carers understand about the term "good enough parenting" and how do they link this with their own experiences and standards?

- How will carers manage the needs of child and parent when they are both children?

- Are they able to ensure that the child remains the paramount concern at all times?

- Do carers have a good understanding of available support systems e.g. Teenage Pregnancy Midwife, Include, Children's Centres, etc ?

- Where do they see these agencies fitting into the assessment process and meeting ongoing support needs of the family?

- If a placement is residential how will the carer encourage the parent to take full care of child?

- Would carers have the ability to intervene if it was felt that the parent was offering inappropriate/risky care?

2. **An ability to work closely with children's families, and others who are important to the child**

- How would carers provide an environment conducive to a good assessment?

- How does the carer see their role in term of working with the "other" parent /extended family?

- Does the carer have the ability to assess the impact external factors have on the parent's ability to care for and protect their child?

- How would the carer build in time and use reflection/feedback with the parent?

3. **An ability to set appropriate boundaries, and manage children's behaviour within these without the use of physical or other inappropriate punishment**

- How will the carer set down clear boundaries with the parent? Is the carer clear about boundaries within the home that are non-negotiable and negotiable? Do they value the use of the planning meeting and written agreements and are they able to work to these?

- Is the carer able to recognise how their own behaviour/standards/values may impact on the assessment?

- Can the carer demonstrate an understanding of the reasons underlying various behaviours and be open to exploring different perspectives?

- What is the carer's attitude to different behaviours and the modification techniques that can be used in different situations?

- What does the carer understand by role modelling and what will this mean for all members of the family when undertaking this type of task?

- Is the carer committed to finding creative and innovative ways of assessing? Are they able to use a range of tools and assess which ones would be useful to address certain issues?

4. **A knowledge of normal child development and an ability to listen and communicate with children appropriate to their age and understanding**

- In terms of assessing parents it may be that you are working with a parent who is a "child" – how would you assess their level of development whilst conducting an assessment of their parenting?

- Will the carer be able to break down the task of parenting and communicate this to the parent?

- Does the carer have a range of communication skills?

- Does the carer have an ability to seek out other fostering services for advice/support for themselves and/or parent around issues of child development?

UNDERSTAND HEALTH AND SAFETY, AND HEALTHY CARE/ KEEP CHILDREN AND YOUNG PEOPLE SAFE FROM HARM

1. **An ability to ensure that the children/young people are cared for in a home where they are safe from harm and abuse**

    - Does the carer understand what is necessary to provide a safe environment for the assessment to take place?

    - Does the carer have an awareness of the legislation, policies and guidelines that underpin practice in the child care arena?

    - What does the carer identify as safeguarding issues for these types of placements? Are they able to integrate these into a Safe Care Plan?

    - How will the carer assess, encourage and enable the parent to take responsibility for their own and their child's health and safety?

2. **An ability to help children keep themselves safe from harm or abuse and to know how to seek help if their safety is threatened**

    - Be aware of the skills and knowledge parents need to keep themselves and their children safe from harm and abuse and have the ability to assess risk.

    - Help parents develop skills through experience, discussion and observation of carer as a role model.

    - Encourage parents to reflect on how they can identify safe and unsafe situations and engage protective strategies.

    - Help parents identify their own support networks which they can access when necessary.

    - How will the carer work with the parent regarding self-protection skills?

KNOW HOW TO COMMUNICATE EFFECTIVELY

1. **An ability to work with other professional people and contribute to the department's planning for the child/young person**

    - Does the carer have a commitment to child-centred practice?

    - How will the carer manage and prioritise the needs of two "children" whilst keeping the baby's needs paramount?

    - Does the carer understand the importance of planning, exploring and using a range of interventions and being able to evaluate these?

- Is the carer able to support the parent in contributing to their child's plans?

- Are they able to advocate on behalf of the child and/or the parent when necessary?

2. **An ability to communicate effectively**

- Is the carer able to communicate and articulate the findings of their assessments to parents and members of the team involved?

- Is the carer able to communicate their findings in a report that is clear, well balanced and analytical?

- Can the carer use a range of communication skills to engage the parent in a good working relationship?

- Does the carer have good negotiation skills?

- How does the carer feel they will be able to manage if interpreting facilities are needed during the assessment?

3. **An ability to keep information confidential**

- An ability to use information appropriately?

- Able to provide information on a need to know basis?

- Have an understanding and commitment to maintaining confidentiality?

- Is the carer able to provide space for the parents to store information safely and securely?

4. **An ability to promote equality, diversity and value the rights of individuals and groups within society**

- What is the carer's understanding of the discrimination faced by some of the parents they may be working with i.e. teenage parents, parents with drug and alcohol issues, parents with a learning difficulty, etc?

- What is the carer's understanding of how cultural and racial issues influence parenting?

- Is the carer able to critically evaluate their own attitudes and values and how they will impact on their role as a parent and child assessment carer?

- Does the carer have a commitment to the concept that all individuals have rights?

- Does the carer understand, promote and celebrate difference?

- Does the carer accept that all parents and children should be guaranteed the same quality of service?

- Is the carer able to challenge racism, discrimination and inequality?

DEVELOP YOURSELF

1. **An ability to appreciate how personal experiences have affected themselves and their families and the impact fostering is likely to have on them all**

    - What is their experience of being parented/parenting?

    - Is the carer able to explore other attitudes towards and understanding of other methods/styles of parenting?

    - Do all family members understand what is involved in being parent/child assessment foster carers?

    - Can they recognise their own limits?

2. **An ability to have people and links within the community which provide support**

    - Is the carer able to seek out support?

    - Does that carer have a commitment to a multi-agency approach to working with families?

    - Is the carer able to make links with services in the community?

    - Is the carer committed to attending monthly support groups?

3. **An ability to use training opportunities and to improve skills**

    - Does the carer value training?

    - Is the carer able to identify own training needs?

    - Is the carer committed to attending training?

    - Is the carer open to other forms of training i.e. shadowing, observing, etc?

4. **An ability to sustain positive relationships and maintain effective functioning through periods of stress**

    - Is the carer able to identify when the placement is in crisis and be open and honest with the team involved?

    - How will the carer retain a positive working relationship with the parent through periods of stress?

    - Does the carer have strategies to employ when experiencing stressful episodes e.g. recognising a need for time out either for parent or self?

    - Is the carer able to identify their own and their family's support needs?

© Leeds Social Care 2011

Appendix 3
Form F Addendum – TACT

TACT
Fostering & Adoption

Form F – Addendum/Addition to Annual Review

Child and Parent – approval to foster

Presented to Fostering Panel on: (date)	

Foster Carers Name(s):	
Address:	

1. Introduction (Briefly outline any experience of fostering to date and include an account of their decision to apply to do Child and Parent placements.)

2. Accommodation/equipment (Describe the suitability of the accommodation for Child and Parent placements and also confirm that carers will be able to provide all the necessary equipment and be able to respond without delay to a referral.)

3. Knowledge and experience of care of babies (Experience of raising one's own child/ children is generally required.)

4. Understanding of attachment and how to promote/ support this between parent and infant (Carers should be able to give examples of how early attachment might be encouraged.)

5. Understanding of role (Carers must understand that their role is to enable, assist and oversee the care of the baby in most cases, but not to take over. When the care being given does not meet the higher standards of the carer, the balance between overseeing and intervening can be difficult to achieve.)

6. Background of parents (Carers must understand that parents may present with a range of difficulties including, mental health problems, drug misuse or learning difficulties. Carers will need to apply a non judgemental approach in working with parents.)

7. Relationship with the parent (Parents may not always be teenagers and will sometimes be adults in their 30s. The presence of another adult living in the household brings about a very different dynamic, and potentially, tensions that are different to that of regular fostering. The impact of this on all family members, including carers' own children, must be considered.)

8. Safeguarding (The carer must consider how to deal with the refusal of the parent to take advice being given or when the care being provided by the parent is unsafe.)

9. Demands on foster carer (Carers are often expected to offer 24 hour support e.g. supervising night feeds and on occasions carers may have the baby in their own room. The demands are therefore different to regular fostering.)

10. Ability to work in partnership with professionals
(Up to 20 professionals may be involved at any one time in working together in Child and Parent cases – ability to work as part of a team is therefore essential.)

11. Ability to keep accurate records (Child and Parent carers will be expected to keep accurate, detailed and objective recordings of the parents' care of the child and overall functioning, which may be used as a vital element of the overall assessment and be used as evidence in court proceedings. These recordings will need to be made available to the court from the start of the placement – Carers should be shown good examples of how information should be recorded.)

12. Preparedness to give evidence in court (Carers must be prepared to give evidence in court which may be under cross-examination.)

13. Living with uncertainty (Plans for the child and timescales may change with very little notice which can be difficult for carers to live with – Carers' support needs should be considered.)

(blank box)

14. Training (It is recognised that carers may have additional training needs in relation to some of the above areas. Please identify any additional training needs. **NB Carers will be expected to attend the Child and Parent training as part of the requirement of taking such placements.**)

15. Recommendation (Please sum up the reason for your recommendation)

Name of assessing social worker	
Signature of assessing social worker	
Date	

© The Adolescent and Child's Trust (TACT), 2010

Appendix 4

Training for current and prospective Child and Parent foster carers – TACT

DAY 1 – Legislative Framework

- An overview of the Public Law Outline, including brief background to legislation and implications for foster carers, their link workers and Local Authority social workers

- An introduction to the family courts, including legal outcomes

- Courtroom players

- Courtroom skills including rules and the giving of evidence

- Confidentiality and sub-judice

DAY 2 – Assessment Skills

- The use of written contracts, ground rules, expectations etc

- Principles of good quality evidence-based assessments

- Understanding the Assessment Framework

DAY 3 – Assessment Skills (Continued)

- The use of observation as evidence

- Making sense of non verbal communication

- Parenting styles

- Understanding the importance of attachment

DAY 4 – Report Writing Skills

- Analytical writing skills and report writing

- How, what and when to record accurately

- Data Protection Act 1998

DAY 5 – Working with Parents

- The use of role modelling
- Value judgements and anti-discriminatory practice
- Parents with specific learning, communication, racial and religious needs
- Communication styles
- Contact issues

DAY 6 – Looking After Yourself

- Keeping yourself and your family safe
- Back up and support
- Dealing with concerns
- Coping with stress

Training Structure

1. It is proposed that the training will take place over a six – eight-week timescale, with delegates attending one day each week. An extra day may be added to the existing programme, if deemed necessary by TACT in conjunction with the trainer.

2. It is envisaged that there will be a mix of social workers and foster carers in attendance and could include administrative staff if need be. The programme will include some reading, exercises and reflection to do as 'homework' which will be fed back during the following training session.

3. Each training day will commence at 10.00 and finish at 4.30 with a half hour lunch break. Actual training time will equate to six hours each day. Certificates of attendance will be provided.

4. Training sessions will include presentations, case studies, discussion, group work, quizzes and video material.

5. During one of the training days, a health professional will deliver a half-day session on child development.

© *The Adolescent and Child's Trust (TACT), 2010.*

Appendix 5
Parent and Child Referral Form (Parts 1 and 2) – Fostering People

fosteringpeople
changing lives **together**

Entered on: Database: Y / N Ref No: .... Excel: Y / N

Date of Ref: ....

FOSTERING PEOPLE – REFERRAL FORM PART 1 – FOR PARENT AND CHILD PLACEMENT

Name of Referrer:		**Authority:**	
Job Title:		**Branch:**	
Telephone Number:		**Fax Number:**	
Social Worker:		**Tel No:**	
Address:		**Fax No:**	
Team Manager:		**Tel No:**	
Name of Parent(s):		**DOB:**	
Home/Current Address:			

Name & Address of Person(s) With Parental Responsibility: (If Parent Is Under 18)			
Expected Date of Confinement:		Date Placement Required:	
Name of Hospital Booked:			
Legal Status:	☐ Accommodated ☐ Interim Care Order ☐ Other ☐ EPO ☐ Full Care Order		
Parent on CPR Y/N:		Category:	☐ Physical ☐ Sexual ☐ Emotional ☐ Neglect
Ethnic Origin:		Nationality:	
Religion:		Language: (if not English Language)	

Name Of Child(ren): (If Applicable)		M/F DOB	
		M/F DOB	
		M/F DOB	
Current Address:			

Ethnic Origin:		Nationality:	
Religion:		Language: (if not English Language)	
Does anyone, apart From the Mother have Parental Responsibility for the Child (ren) Yes / No		Name: Address:	

Legal Status: Accommodated ☐ Interim Care Order ☐ Full Care Order ☐ EPO ☐

Other ☐ NB Either Parent or Child must be LAC

Child on CPR YES/NO

Category: Physical ☐ Sexual ☐ Emotional ☐ Neglect ☐ Failure to thrive ☐

PLACEMENT DETAILS FOR MATCHING

Present Placement:	☐ LA Foster service ☐ Ind.Residential ☐ IFA ☐ LA Secure ☐ LA Residential ☐ Birth Family ☐ Other:
Length in this Placement:	
Amount of Placements in:	LA Foster service: IFA: LA Residential: Ind.Residential: LA Secure: Birth Family: Other:
Reason for Placement Move:	
What are the Short-term Plans for the Parent & Child?	
What are the Long-term Plans for the Parent & Child?	
Are there any Court Hearings (Civil or Criminal) Pending? Y/N: (If Yes Please Give Details)	

PARENT AND CHILD FOSTERING

Request any Current:	☐ Care Plans ☐ Pathway Plan ☐ Court Directions ☐ LAC Review ☐ Core assessment ☐ Case Conference Minutes ☐ Connexions Assessments ☐ Health Assessment ☐ Education Statements ☐ Other Assessment ☐ Psychological		
Preferred Location:			
Type of Foster Home to Meet the Needs of Placement (E.G. All Female, No Pets]			
What Wishes/Requests Does the Parent have Regarding their Foster Placement?			
Will The Current Partner of the Parent Be Involved During The Placement?			
Background: (i.e. Reasons For Placement)			
Behavioural Issues:			
Offending Behaviour: Known Offences	☐ TDA ☐ Bail Conditions ☐ Violence ☐ Burglary ☐ Court Conditions ☐ Theft ☐ Curfew ☐ Other ☐ Don't Know		
Please Specify:			
Any Outstanding Court Appearances Y/N:		Please Specify:	
YOT Worker:		Tel. No:	

© Fostering People, 2011

Appendix 6
Risk Assessment for Parent and Child Placements – Pathway Care

PATHWAY CARE
Leading to a Better Future

FAMILIES FIRST
Parenting Assessment

Name of Parent(s) and Child(ren) being assessed:
Address:
Name of foster parent(s):

Current Situation (including legal status):
Past History *(to be completed by the Local Authority Social Worker)*
Are there any known previous prosecutions and/or known police involvement? YES ☐ NO ☐   **If YES, please specify.**

Have there been any violent incidents directed at people? YES ☐ NO ☐ **If YES, please specify.**
Have there been any incidents where weapons of any sort were involved? YES ☐ NO ☐ **If YES, please specify.**
Have there been any incidents of damage to property? YES ☐ NO ☐ **If YES, please specify.**
Have there been any incidents of arson? YES ☐ NO ☐ **If YES, please specify.**
Have there been any incidents where verbal aggression or threats have been displayed? YES ☐ NO ☐ **If YES, please specify.**
Have there been any incidents of self-harming? YES ☐ NO ☐ **If YES, please specify.**
Have there been any incidents of sexual abuse/sexualised behaviour? YES ☐ NO ☐ **If YES, please specify.**
Is the parent known to be racist? YES ☐ NO ☐

Does the parent have any possessions which might cause concern e.g. penknife, matches, alcohol etc? YES ☐ NO ☐
Risk Management Plan (To be completed by Families First in consultation with LA SW)
At the time of admission is the parent agitated, upset or distressed? YES ☐ NO ☐
Does the information given indicate that there is a significant risk posed to the child, parent, carers, carer's children or visitors to the home? YES ☐ NO ☐
What are the procedures/contingencies to be followed in the event of incident/ occurrence? **Procedures considered:**   **Procedures agreed:**
Who has been involved in developing this plan?
Are there differences of opinion about the plan? YES ☐ NO ☐ **If YES, please specify.**
Signed (SW) **Signed (FF)**   **Date:**

Appendix 7
Adult Risk Assessment for Parent and Child Placement – Somerset County Council

ADULT RISK ASSESSMENT FOR PARENT AND CHILD PLACEMENT		
Parent's Details:		

Name:	DOB:	Ethnicity:	Date:

Primary Address:

Section A – Parent being placed

Please tick the relevant boxes	YES	NO
Is there a current Police check available in respect of the parent?	☐	☐
If so, please provide details:		
If there is not a current Police check, please ask the parent if they have any offences. **For placing a parent and child in a foster home we require information about any offences they have committed or are charged with**		
Does the parent have a history of allegations against adults of a physical/sexual nature?	☐	☐
Description of behaviour:		
Does the parent target males?	☐	☐
Does the parent target females?	☐	☐
Description of behaviour		
Is the parent verbally aggressive?	☐	☐

Description of behaviour (please note known triggers):		
Has the parent ever been physically aggressive?	☐	☐
Description of behaviour (please note known triggers and if there was an intention to harm/hurt):		
Has the parent ever been sexually aggressive?	☐	☐
Description of behaviour (please note known triggers):		
Has, or does, the parent substance misuse?	☐	☐
Details of substance misuse (please note known triggers):		
Are there aspects to the parent's mental health or emotional wellbeing that affect their behaviour?	☐	☐
Description of behaviour (please note known triggers):		
Does the parent have a known health condition that could present a risk?	☐	☐
Details of condition and risk:	☐	☐
Section B – Partners/Family Members/Associates of Parent being placed		
In some circumstances the parent being placed may have a partner/ex partner/family member/associates who have posed and continue to pose a risk to them and the child/children. In these circumstances the following information is required before a placement can be agreed:		
Please provide Name, Date of Birth and Address of the person(s) who is a risk:		
Please provide full details of the nature of the risk to the parent and child and description of behaviour:		
Does the person have a lifestyle or offences that may pose a risk to a foster placement if that person were to have contact (authorised or unauthorised) with the parent and child in placement?	☐	☐
If so, please provide details:		
Should the placement address be treated as confidential?	☐	☐
Should a Police Communications marker be placed on the foster carer's home?	☐	☐

Appendix 8
Leaflets for parents and professionals – Somerset, West Sussex and Brighton and Hove

Somerset, West Sussex and Brighton and Hove have each developed information leaflets for parents which all set out information on how parent and child fostering works in the specific schemes set up by their agency and the roles and responsibilities of all involved. Somerset has an equivalent leaflet for professionals. These can be viewed at www.baaf.org.uk/bookshop/Parentandchild.

Appendix 9
Parent and Baby Foster Placement Set up Meeting Template – Brighton and Hove City Council

Name of Parent in placement:

Child's D.O.B:

Name of Social Worker for Child:

Name of carer:

Name of Social Worker for carer:

Attended by:

Chair of meeting:

Date of Meeting:

1. **Objectives of the placement**

    > Detail key issues that have resulted in the plan for a Parent & Baby foster placement.
    > What does the parent need to achieve before a rehabilitation plan in the community can commence?

2. **Expectations of the foster carer**

Detail the teaching and assessment tasks required and the level of supervision needed.

Are there any cultural, ethnic, religious, language, gender, sexuality issues, or disability needs for either parent or child?

3. Recording

Detail expectations of the foster carer in terms of recording and how this will be shared with the parent and kept under review.

4. Expectations of the parents within the foster carers' home

Detail specific responsibilities for the baby, including all aspects of the baby's care during the day and night. Are there any restrictions on the amount of time the parent can spend alone with the baby in the bedroom? N.B. there must be no bed sharing at night.

Detail expectations of the parent within the foster home for domestic tasks, such as washing, shopping, cooking, budgeting.

5. Financial arrangements between carer and parent

Detail financial arrangements between parent and carer. Is the parent in receipt of Income Support? Any claims need to be on an individual rather than a joint basis.

6. Parent's time out of placement

Detail agreement in relation to any time off that the parent can have from the responsibilities of caring for the baby, or to attend other assessment appointments, or unsupervised time with the baby outside of the home.

7. **Health issues**

> Detail any specific issues in relation to the parent and baby including attendance at appointments and liaison with key professionals. Include storage of medication/prescription drugs. Reaffirm expectations about alcohol use, smoking or use of other substances.

8. **Contact details**

> Contact arrangements both for others with the baby and contact the parent can have with others without the baby. Include direct contact meetings as well as indirect contact via phone, text, etc.

9. **Assessment work**

> How work within the foster placement will fit with other assessment work that is planned or underway, and timescales for the assessment work with any key court dates. Detail other assessment work and who is undertaking this.

10. **Length of placement**

> Anticipated length of the placement

> Under what circumstances would the placement be terminated, and what care arrangements would be made for the child if the parent left the placement including the possibility of the baby then moving to a baby only foster placement?
>
> Rehabilitation plan if the placement and assessment work is successful and any work that needs to be undertaken at an early stage in relation to housing needs of the parent, or the need to identify appropriate community resources – and who will have responsibility for this.
>
> There needs to be a clear exit plan, and a specific meeting to review the rehabilitation plan.

11. Network meetings

> Plans for establishment of a Network group and Network meetings to be held at least at 6-weekly intervals. Role of network meetings alongside LAC reviews.

12. Concerns

> What should happen if the parent has any concerns or issues about the placement?

> What will happen if the carer has concerns about any aspect of the parent's behaviour or their care of the child?

13. Foster carer commitments

> Any plans to cover any outstanding commitments foster carers have such as key training events:

15. Other Issues

> e.g use of photography/social networking sites/confidentiality of the address of the carer
>
> The parent is prohibited from placing photographs of the foster carer's home circumstances onto his/her Facebook page.
> It is expected that the carer's supervising social worker and the child's social worker regularly inspect the parental bedroom.

A date for a Review of the placement needs to be set 6 weeks from date of set up meeting.

These minutes do need to be sent or emailed out to the foster carer ideally 48 hours after the set up meeting.

Appendix 10
Areas to consider when making a Parent and Baby Assessment Placement – East Sussex County Council

Budgeting/Household tasks:

- Usually with new placements there is a settling in period when the foster carers are willing to do all the cooking, cleaning and washing to allow the parent to concentrate purely on the baby for the first week or two. This needs to be negotiated and re-considered at each weekly meeting.

- Will there be any financial assistance, and from whom, if their benefits are not in place?

- What will the parent/s be responsible for buying, considering they will often be in receipt of benefits?

- What meals will the parent/s be responsible for buying and preparing and when will it be convenient for the specific household for them to undertake this task? Will they eat separately to other family members?

- How will their budgeting skills be monitored?

Supervision

- Outline that the parent/s is/are fully responsible for the care and stimulation for their baby and consider the occasions when foster carer is likely to intervene.

- When can the parent/s go out on their own; for how long; and what preparations does s/he need to make regarding their baby beforehand?

- Can the parent/s go out on their own with the baby and if so, are there any restrictions in regards to who they can meet up with and where they can go?

- Can the parent/s be left on their own in the home with or without their baby for any length of period e.g. school run?

- If the parent/s is/are not to be left in the placement on their own with the baby, what commitments does the foster carer have which the parent will need to accompany them to (i.e. school run, after school activities, dentist/hospital appointments etc)? What will need to happen if the parent is not ready – will the foster carer need to take the baby and leave the parent at home?

- Will the foster carer need to observe night feeds and if so for how long? Sometimes this can be helpful for the parent especially since they are in a new house and may not know where everything is kept.

- Exactly what does the foster carer need to observe? Feeding, bathing, changing? Is it the expectation that the parent will inform the carer when they are going to undertake these tasks? Does the foster carer need to be physically present at all times or within earshot? It is important that this is clarified.

- What will the arrangements be to register the baby's birth especially if both parents' names are to be on the certificate? How can this be managed safely if they wish to take the baby with them?

Contact

- Who will be supervising any contact with other family members, and will this form part of the assessment?

- Is there anyone that the parent/s is/are advised against having contact with?

- If there is a named person who has been identified as presenting a risk to the placement or child and they were to turn up at the placement, what will the foster carers be advised to do?

- Are there any restrictions on phone contact? Are parents expected to solely use their mobile phones? Is there a time by which incoming phone calls will cause difficulties within the placement?

Recordings

- What recordings are expected from the foster carer and how often are these to be shared with the Social Worker and Family Resource Centre? If they are not completed electronically, who will be responsible for copying these to all those who need to have sight of them?

- How often and when will the recordings be shared with the parent/s? The parents should be encouraged to sign and include any comments they may wish to make.

Possessions

- What equipment would the parent like to bring to the placement?

- What equipment will the parent need to buy/borrow?

Assessment

- Where and when will this start?

- When is the agreement meeting likely to take place if not already held?

- The parent/s will be expected to attend and engage in all sessions arranged at the family resource centre. Will they be expected to make their own way? If not, who will transport them and will this continue throughout the placement? This will need to be reviewed at each weekly meeting.

- If the foster carer is expected to care for the baby, on such occasions the parent/s will be expected to make sufficient preparation for this to occur smoothly e.g. prepared any feeds which may be needed in advance.

General responsibilities

- What areas in the house will the parent/s need to be responsible to keep clean, and who will monitor this?

- How often will the social worker/assessment team monitor the parent's bedroom and will this be unannounced? What are the expectations of the foster carers and parents in regards to this?

- If the parent/s is/are on any medication, what is it, what are the amounts and how will this be managed within the placement including where the medication will be kept?

- If the parent/s have their own car, what checks may be needed if they are wishing to transport their child/ren?

- What outstanding appointments does the parent have which we need to consider transport and child-care for in the next few weeks including health, court/solicitor appointments?

- What other professionals are involved with the parent/s?

- Are there any housing issues which will need to be addressed i.e. securing of their home, collecting post etc.?

- What are the consequences of not keeping to the agreement or particular areas within it?

© East Sussex County Council, 2011

Appendix 11
Child and Parent Placement Agreement – TACT

The following principles and practice guidelines underpin the TACT Parent/Child placement service

- Assessments are reliant on good relationships between the foster carer/assessor, the parent, and the wider team, working in a climate of collaboration, trust and building on parents' strengths.

- The focus of the placement is to enable and support the parent in caring for her/his child as independently as possible. Thus parents will be helped in developing not only their parenting and nurturing abilities, but also those skills needed for independent living, including responsible citizenship and positive self-esteem.

- The child is the responsibility of the parent in placement.

- The foster carer is ultimately responsible for ensuring the child's basic needs are met should the parent fail to do this.

- The foster carer must report any child care or safeguarding concerns immediately to the child's social worker and to the TACT Supervising Social Worker.

- The parent must adhere to any agreements and conditions established at the pre placement meeting.

- There should be honesty and transparency in the foster carer's recording and observations.

- TACT will provide the Local Authority with information and assessment in an agreed form in respect of parenting capacity and the relationship between parent and child.

- This assessment will be in the context of work with a team of professionals who support the parent.

- The assessment is intended to contribute to the decision-making process for the child in that it identifies needs and solutions, aids in formulating an action plan and clarifies timescales, priorities, objectives and responsibilities.

● The assessment will be a dynamic but robust process which in itself is frequently therapeutic and empowering.

SECTION 1

A. CHILD'S DETAILS

Forenames		Surname	
Preferred name		Gender	
Date of birth			
Legal status while looked after			
Name of person/s with parental responsibilities			
Address			
Tel no.			
Ethnicity			
Linguistic needs			

Identified special needs	
Cultural needs	

	Service User Personal Reference Number	

Is child undergoing any medical treatment currently? If YES please detail		Does the child have any outstanding appointments? Please give details	
Does the child have any disabilities?	YES / NO	If YES, what needs arise from the disabilities?	

Does child require any special diet (including cultural requirements) or feeding routine? If YES, details:	YES / NO	Has the child had a hearing test?	YES / NO
Are the child's immunisations up to date?	YES / NO	Who holds the Red Book?	
Does the child have adequate clothing at commencement of placement?		Does the child's hair require any special treatment? Give details	Does the child's skin require any special treatment?

CONTACT

What arrangements are made for the child to have contact with their mother, father, siblings, grandparents and/or significant others? How will introductions to foster carers be made?	
Have any court orders been made, relating to this?	

Is a risk assessment necessary? By what date will it be done?	YES / NO	Who is paying for contact arrangements?	

Will foster carers need to provide transport in order to facilitate contact?	Is the distance involved greater than 15 miles?
YES / NO	YES / NO If YES who will fund this?

B.1 MOTHER'S DETAILS

Forenames		Surname	
Preferred name		In placement with child yes or no	
Date of birth		Legal status if LAC	

Future home address	
Telephone number(s)	
Ethnicity	
Linguistic needs	
Cultural needs	
Special needs including disability	

Service User Personal Reference Number	

B.2 FURTHER DETAILS IF MOTHER IS LOOKED AFTER — full details on Mother's PP agreement (If 18 or over go straight to B.3)

EDUCATION

Last school attended/college/employment	
Proposed new school/college/employment	
Who will negotiate the above?	
Arrangements for care of child whilst mother is in education/employment	

HEALTH

What is the mother's general health?					
Does mother have any outstanding appointments including post natal care?					
Does the mother have any disabilities?	**YES / NO**	**If YES, what needs arise from the disabilities?**			
Does mother have psychiatric/psychological appointments?			**Does the mother receive D.L.A?**	**YES / NO**	

Does mother require any special diet (including cultural requirement)? **If YES, details**	
Who has responsibility for ensuring mother's routine health needs are met (appointments, dentist, diet, etc) i.e. her own mother/foster carer/ other	

CONTACT

What arrangements are made for mother to have contact with her own mother, father, siblings, grandparents and/or significant others? How will introductions to foster carers be made?			
Have any court orders been made relating to this?			
Is a risk assessment necessary? By what date will it be done?	**YES / NO**	**Who is paying for mother's own contact arrangements?**	

Are there any limitations on telephone contact including mobile phones?	YES / NO	Will foster carers need to provide transport in order to facilitate contact?	YES / NO
Is the distance involved greater than 15 miles?	YES / NO	If YES who will fund this?	

B.3 FURTHER DETAILS IF MOTHER IS 18 or over i.e. NOT LOOKED AFTER

EDUCATION

Last school attended/ college/employment	
Proposed new school/ college/employment	
Who will negotiate the above?	
Arrangements for care of child whilst mother is in education/employment	
Does mother have a learning disability?	

HEALTH

What is the mother's general health?			
Does mother have any special health needs and/ or allergies?			
Is mother undergoing any medical treatment currently? If YES please detail		Does mother have any outstanding appointments including post natal care? Give details	
Does the mother have any disabilities and if so what are the implications for the placement?			

Who has responsibility for ensuring mother's routine health needs are met (appointments, dentist, diet, etc) i.e. mother herself/foster carer/other?	

C. FATHER'S DETAILS (If father is also LAC section B.2 can be cut and pasted here)

Forenames		**Surname**	
Preferred name		**Date of Birth**	
Contact arrangements if not in placement e.g. where, when, supervised by			
Future home address			
Telephone number(s)			
Ethnicity			
Linguistic needs			
Cultural needs			
Special needs including disability			

D. PROFESSIONAL CONTACTS details (name address, e-mail, tel no)

G.P. for child	
G.P. for parent	
Health visitor	
Support worker	
Mental health services	
Drug and alcohol services	
Probation/YOT	

L.A. Social worker for child	
L.A. Social worker for parent	
L.A. Team Manager	
Other	

E. ROLES AND RESPONSIBILITIES of other professionals

L.A.S.W. part to be played in assessment, tasks identified **Has all requested documentation been received? If not when will outstanding reports etc be provided?**	
G. P. for child	
G.P. for parent	
Health visitor **Frequency of visits** **Focus of involvement**	
Other health worker e.g. dietician **Frequency of visits** **Focus of involvement**	
Support worker **Frequency of visits** **Contribution to assessment**	
Mental health services **Level of involvement** **Contact arrangements** **Contribution to assessment**	
Drug and alcohol services **Level of involvement** **Expectations of service user** **Contribution to assessment**	

Probation/YOT worker **Level of involvement** **Any outstanding court dates** **Contribution to assessment**	

Placement Type **Who will prepare the assessment** **report? Give contact details** **L.A.S.W.** **TACT foster carer** **TACT independent assessor** **TACT social worker** **L.A. appointed worker** *NB – focus of placement should* *not be changed without prior* *discussion with TACT*	
Placement plan **Duration** **Is ongoing care required for child** **should parent leave placement?** **Is support required for parent** **and child when independence** **achieved? If so for how long?** **(charged at TACT hourly sessional** **rates)**	
Introductions *(what are arrangements for* *introducing child and /or parent* *to foster family?)*	
Risk factors *(are there any specific safety* *issues?)*	
Arrangement for placing **authority social worker visits** *(Inc. frequency)*	

F. ROLES AND REPONSIBILITIES OF FOSTER CARER(S)

Level of supervision of parent and child (day/evening /night). Specify when and if foster carer should enter bedroom	
Has carer received all information about parent's health, any drug or alcohol misuse, any risk factors, and full relevant background information? If not, how and when is this to be provided?	
What are the carer's responsibilities re food and clothing, and cleaning of parent/ child room?	
Will carers provide any equipment and if so what?	
What babysitting and day time care is the carer to provide?	
Who will provide support to the carer e.g. time out?	

G. RESPONSIBILITIES AND EXPECTATIONS OF PARENT

Does the parent understand that smoking and drug taking including alcohol is not permitted in the carer's home?	
What food and clothing is the parent expected to supply?	
What meals etc is the parent expected to prepare?	
What are the parent's responsibilities re washing and cleaning?	

What are the arrangements for the parent entertaining visitors?	
Does the parent understand that the foster carer is expected to report any concerns and record observations – these will be shared with the parent	

What are the agreed sanctions should the parent not comply with any agreements?	
Are there any specific goals for the parent to achieve e.g. attendance at clinic, child's weight gain, sorting benefits?	

SECTION 2

TACT DETAILS

Address	
Tel no.	
Agency contact person	
Tel no.	
Supervising Social Worker *(for liaison purposes on the placement)*	
Financial/Accounts contact person	
Address	
Tel no.	

SECTION 3

PLACING AUTHORITY'S DETAILS

Name of LA	
Social worker	
Address	
Tel no.	email
Out of hours tel no.	

Team manager	
Address	
Tel no.	email

LOCAL AUTHORITY CONTACT FOR CONTRACTUAL ISSUES

Name		Job title	
Address (if different from above)			
Tel no.		email	

LOCAL AUTHORITY CONTACT FOR FINANCIAL ISSUES

Name		Job title	
Address *(if different from above)*			
Tel no.		email	

SECTION 4

COMMENCEMENT/REVIEW DETAILS

This Placement Agreement shall commence			
On:		To:	

REVIEW DETAILS

Any change in the Care, Health and/or Education needs of the child/young person agreed within the Placement meeting or Statutory Review should then be considered by the allocated Social Worker in a review of this Placement Agreement

Next statutory review date: (complete as appropriate)		or within:	

SECTION 5

THE ADOLESCENT & CHILDREN'S TRUST AGREES

1. That TACT will supply all information specified in Schedule 3, The Fostering Services Regulations 2002;[1] to enable the Responsible Authority to make an approval of a foster placement in accordance with Regulation 40(6) of the Fostering Services Regulations 2002 and Regulation 40(6) of the Fostering Services (Wales) Regulations 2003.

2. That TACT will undertake all consultations with other authorities that have children in placement, to seek consent to the placement of a further child. Fostering Services Regulations 2002 Reg. 34(2)(b) and Fostering Services (Wales) Regulations 2003 Reg. 34(2)(b).

3. That TACT will notify the relevant area authority of the proposal to place a child with TACT carers on behalf of the Responsible Authority to which this agreement refers, in accordance with paragraph 34(2) Fostering Services Regulations 2002 and paragraph 34(2) Fostering Services (Wales) Regulations 2003.

4. To undertake a review of approval of the foster carers at intervals of not more than a year, and provide a copy of any notice given under Reg. 29(10) of the Fostering Services Regulations 2002 to the carers and to all placing authorities and Reg. 29(10) of the Fostering Services (Wales) Regulations 2003.

5. To undertake the supervision of this placement and make contact with the child and foster carers. TACT Supervising Social Workers will spend time alone with the child unless the child, being of sufficient age and understanding to do so, refuses. This is in addition to any visit the social worker may make in accordance with Regulation 35(1) of the Fostering Services Regulations 2002 and Regulations 35(1) of the Fostering Services (Wales) Regulations 2003.

---

[1] This form was drafted prior to the publication of the Fostering Services Regulations 2011

6. To make a written report of each and every contact in accordance with Regulation 35(3) of the Fostering Services Regulations 2002 and Regulation 35(3) of the Fostering Services (Wales) Regulations 2003.

7. To provide a written agreement with the foster carer(s) to whom this agreement refers in accordance with Regulation 28(5)(b) of the Fostering Services Regulations 2002 and Regulation 28(5)(b) of the Fostering Services (Wales) Regulations 2003.

8. To provide advice, support and assistance to the foster carers to whom this agreement refers over a 24-hour period for each and every day of the placement to which this agreement refers.

9. To provide training for all foster carers associated with TACT with due regard to each individual's training needs assessment.

10. To provide foster carers with access to TACT's Representation and Complaints procedure.

11. That a placement will not be terminated by The Adolescent & Children's Trust without prior discussion or notice.

12. To inform the responsible authority immediately in the event of any concerns about the placement.

13. To maintain the highest standard of child care practice at all times.

14. To review each child care plan at intervals as agreed with the Responsible Authority.

15. To provide for frequent consultation and exchange of information with the Responsible Authority on all aspects of the child's progress and development.

16. To ensure that TACT foster carers comply with the Foster carer Agreement (known as TACT's Foster Carer Agreement) and the responsible authority's plans for the child(ren).

17. To furnish reports as required to the Responsible Authority.

SECTION 6

PARTIES TO THE ARRANGEMENT

The Service Purchaser and Service Provider agree that the terms of the Pre-Placement Contract

date [   ]

and made between the parties shall apply to this placement

This Placement Agreement is signed and agreed by the following:

	Name	Signature	Date
On behalf of the Service Provider Authorised Representative			
Foster Carers			
Parent(s)			
On behalf of the Service Purchaser Authorised Officer			

© The Adolescent and Children's Trust (TACT), 2010

Appendix 12
Placement Contract – Pathway Care

PATHWAY CARE
Leading to a Better Future

FAMILIES FIRST
Parenting Assessment

PLACEMENT CONTRACT

Name of child: YYYYYY

Name of parent(s): XXXXXX

Placement with:

Placement start date:

Planned end date:

TERMS OF THE PLACEMENT

- XXXX can only bring drugs into the placement given to him/her by his/her GP or bought from the chemist. He/She needs to tell the carer what medicine he/she has and agree where he/she should to keep it

- XXXX can not bring alcohol into the placement.

- Smoking is not allowed inside the house. XXXX can smoke in the garden.

- Pathway Care might ask the assessment to end if XXXX threatens or hits anyone else in the placement.

- A baby monitor will be used at night so that the carers can tell that everything is going well.

- XXXX may not take YYYY away from the placement on their own until it is agreed at a review by Pathway Care and the child's social worker.

- The carer will offer up to four hours babysitting every week so that XXXX can have some time to him/herself.

- XXXX should be dressed in day or night clothes whenever he/she is with anyone else.

- XXXX should not tell anyone else where she is living without the carer's permission.

- XXXX can use the carer's telephone to contact anyone in connection with the assessment (social worker, health visitor, solicitor, children's guardian, etc). Any calls to friends or family should be made on own mobile.

- The carer will write down what he/she sees and hears every day. The carer will read what he/she writes to XXXX or let him/her read it for him/herself. XXXX can add his/her own words if he/she wants to. XXXX will then be asked to sign each sheet. Every week the records will be sent to the Local Authority.

- Any specific incidents or breaking of the contract will be recorded and immediately faxed to the Local Authority.

- XXXX has the right to complain if he/she thinks Pathway Care is doing something wrong. He/she can make this complaint in writing or by speaking to Pathway Care or the Local Authority.

- XXXX may be asked to leave the placement if there is:

  a) any physical violence

  b) shouting and making threats to a level that shows XXXX can not control him/herself

  c) any behaviour which makes other people feel frightened

  d) any circumstances which result in Pathway Care believing that YYYY cannot be kept safe

Signed _____ Date _____

Signed _____ Date _____

Social Worker _____

Signed _____ Date _____

Carer _____

Signed _____ Date _____

Pathway Care _____

Appendix 13
Placement Ending Meeting Form – Pathway Care

PATHWAY CARE
Leading to a Better Future

FAMILIES FIRST
Parenting Assessment

Placement Ending Meeting

Carers:

Dates of placement:

Family name of placement:

Legal status: S20   ICO   S38(6)

Family composition:

Major issues identified: LD   MH   Drug/alcohol DV   CL

Previous child(ren) removed   Previous assessment

Assessment recommendation:

Outcome?

What went well during assessment?

What was difficult during the assessment?

What could the carers have done differently?

What could Pathway Care have done differently?

What can the carers take from the assessment to be used for CWDC?

Would the carers like/need further training or support in any area following this assessment?

_____

Future availability of the carers?

_____

Any other comments?

Appendix 14
Parent and Baby Daily Report – West Sussex County Council

Parent and Baby Daily Report

Date:

Completed by:

RECORD OF DAY

> Child's needs: Please consider routine, play/stimulation (games/reading/singing), physical care (nappy changes, bathing, clean clothes, encouraging development) emotional care (attachments, eye contact, smiles, reassurance).

> Parent's presentation: Please consider parent's stability/emotional wellbeing (frame of mind), timekeeping, cleanliness of bedroom, household chores undertaken and personal self-care (showers, teeth/hair and clean clothes).

Budgeting (Any money given, how money managed and planned for).

Preparation of bottles (cleaning/sterilisation)/cooking (who cooked for parent and child, prepared meals, type of food).

Summary of discussion of the day between Foster Carer and Parent (concerns/positives, intervention, skills to work on).

Parent's comments:

Foster Carer:

Signed: Date:

Parent:

Signed: Date:

Family Placement Social Worker:

Signed: Date:

Appendix 15

Observation log for Parent and Child Placement – Kasper Fostering

Kasper
Fostering

Kasper Fostering

Observation log for parent and child placement

BASIC CARE

Providing for child's physical needs, and appropriate medical/dental care. Includes provision of food, drink, warmth, shelter, clean and appropriate clothing and adequate personal hygiene.

STIMULATION

How was the child's learning and intellectual development promoted (e.g. playing with child in age-appropriate way, talking with and responding to the baby's own communications)?

GUIDANCE AND BOUNDARIES

How was adequate guidance demonstrated by the parent/caregiver, including setting boundaries, e.g. was the child(ren) encouraged to explore, problem solve and interact appropriately? In the case of a baby, think about consistent parenting, not over protecting, and therefore allowing baby to explore through play, etc. Key parental tasks are demonstrating and modelling behaviour. Was carer's advice needed/taken?

SAFETY

Ensuring child is protected from harm or danger, including protection from contact with unsafe adults/young people. Recognition of hazards and danger both in the home and elsewhere.

STABILITY

Consistent emotional warmth shown to baby over time and responding to baby in a similar manner to the same behaviour. Parent responses to baby change and develop according to baby's developmental progress (not according to parent's mood).

EMOTIONAL WARMTH

Ensuring baby's emotional needs are met. Showing appropriate physical contact, comfort, and cuddling sufficient to demonstrate warm regard, praise and encouragement.

SUMMARY/ADDITIONAL OBSERVATIONS/Parent's comments.

Sign and date; carer and parent.

Appendix 16
Assessment Framework – TACT

The **Weekly Summary based on Framework for the Assessment of Child in Need and their Families** assesses the following areas:

Child Development Needs

Health: Includes growth and development as well as physical and mental wellbeing. The impact of genetic factors and of any impairment should be considered. Involves receiving appropriate health care when ill, an adequate and nutritious diet, exercise, immunisations where appropriate and developmental checks, dental and optical care and, for older children, appropriate advice and information on issues that have an impact on health, including sex education and substance misuse.

Education: Covers all areas of a child's cognitive development which begins from birth. Includes opportunities: for play and interaction with other children; to have access to books; to acquire a range of skills and interests; to experience success and achievement. Involves an adult interested in education activities, progress and achievements, who takes account of the child's starting point and any special educational needs.

Emotional and Behavioural Development: Concerns the appropriateness of response demonstrated in feelings and actions by a child, initially to parents and caregivers and, as the child grows older, to others beyond the family. Includes nature and quality of early attachments, characteristics of temperament, adaptation to change, response to stress and degree of appropriate self-control.

Identity: Concerns the child's growing sense of self as a separate and valued person. Includes the child's view of self and abilities, self-image and self-esteem, and having a positive sense of individuality. Race, religion, age, gender, sexuality and disability may all contribute to this. Feelings of belonging and acceptance by family, peer group and wider society, including other cultural groups.

Family and Social Relationships: Development of empathy and the capacity to place self in someone else's shoes. Includes a stable and affectionate relationship with parents or caregivers, good relationships with siblings, increasing importance of age-appropriate friendships with peers and other significant persons in the child's life and response of family to these relationships.

Social Presentation: Concerns child's growing understanding of the way in which appearance, behaviour and any impairment are perceived by the outside world and the impression being created. Includes appropriateness of dress for age, gender, culture and religion; cleanliness and personal hygiene; and availability of advice from parents or care-givers about presentation in different settings.

Self Care Skills: Concerns the acquisition by a child of practical, emotional and communication competencies required for increasing independence. Includes early practical skills of dressing and feeding, opportunities to gain confidence and practical skills to undertake activities away from the family and independent living skills as older children. Includes encouragement to acquire social problem-solving approaches. Special attention should be given to the impact of a child's impairment and other vulnerabilities, and on social circumstances affecting these in the development of self-care skills.

The **Weekly Summary for Dimensions of Parenting Capacity** assesses the following areas:

Basic Care: Providing for the child's physical needs, and appropriate medical and dental care. Includes provision of food, drink, warmth, shelter, clean and appropriate clothing and adequate personal hygiene.

Ensuring Safety: Ensuring the child is adequately protected from harm or danger. Includes protection from significant harm or danger, and from contact with unsafe adults/other children and from self-harm. Recognition of hazards and danger both in the home and elsewhere.

Emotional Warmth: Ensuring the child's emotional needs are met and giving the child a sense of being specially valued and a positive sense of own racial and cultural identity. Includes ensuring the child's requirements for secure, stable and affectionate relationships with significant adults, with appropriate sensitivity and responsiveness to the child's needs. Appropriate physical contact, comfort and cuddling sufficient to demonstrate warm regard, praise and encouragement.

Stimulation: Promoting child's learning and intellectual development through encouragement and cognitive stimulation and promoting social opportunities. Includes facilitating the child's cognitive development and potential through interaction, communication, talking and responding to the child's language and questions, encouraging and joining the child's play, and promoting educational opportunities. Enabling the child to experience success and ensuring school attendance or equivalent opportunity. Facilitating child to meet challenges of life.

Guidance and Boundaries: Enabling the child to regulate their own emotions and behaviour. The key parental tasks are demonstrating and modelling appropriate behaviour and control of emotions and interactions with others, and guidance which involves setting boundaries, so that the child is able to develop an internal model of moral values and conscience, and social behaviour appropriate for the society within which they will grow up. The aim is to enable the child to grow into an autonomous adult, holding their own values, and able to demonstrate appropriate behaviour with others rather than having to be dependent on rules outside themselves. This includes not over-protecting children from exploratory and learning experiences. Includes social problem-solving, anger management, consideration for others and effective discipline and shaping of behaviour.

Stability: Providing a sufficiently stable family environment to enable a child to develop and maintain a secure attachment to the primary caregiver(s) in order to ensure optimal development. Includes: ensuring secure attachments are not disrupted, providing consistency of emotional warmth over time and responding in a similar manner to the same behaviour. Parental responses change and develop according to child's developmental progress. In addition, ensuring children keep in contact with important family members and significant others.

© The Adolescent and Children's Trust (TACT), 2010

Appendix 17
Parent and Child Placement Weekly Progress Sheet – Team Fostering

TEAM FOSTERING
PUTTING CHILDREN'S FUTURES FIRST

Ofsted
Outstanding
2007/2008

Team Fostering

Parent and Child Placement – Weekly Progress Sheet

Parent's name: **Child's name:**

1. Parent's responses to the baby's needs:

Feeding
Bathing
Clothing
Routines
Health (e.g. responding to changes, signs and symptoms)

Safety (e.g. checking baby regularly, ensuring proper equipment is used)
Emotional needs (e.g. warmth, affection, responding to crying)
Stimulation (e.g. playing, talking, singing)
Degree of prompting required to meet baby's needs
Ability to cope with stress, e.g. if baby won't settle or accept feeding

Parent's achievements and difficulties in working towards independence:

Budgeting and shopping
Domestic tasks
Relationships with friends and family
Self-care (e.g. eating, sleeping, personal health and hygiene)
Leisure activities

Education/work

General progress within the foster home:

Relationships with carers and carers' family
Willingness to work with plan

Signed: _____ **(Foster carer)**

Date:

Parent's comments:

Signed: _____ **(Parent)**

Date:

© Team Fostering, 2011

Appendix 18
Recording of Assessment for Parent and Baby Placement – Brighton and Hove City Council

Brighton and Hove Fostering and Adoption Service

Recording of Assessment – Parent and baby Placement

Child's name:

Date or Week ending:

Foster carer's name:

Record if/how aspects of parent's care of the baby change or develop over the weeks of placement. Do you need to continue prompting the parent to do these things?

1. Parent's basic care of baby

Feeds – buy appropriate formula, prepare – think ahead, wash hands, clean equipment & sterilise. Recognise & respond promptly when baby hungry, prepare & give appropriate solid food, listen to & follow advice? Comment on how baby is fed – is it a nurturing warm experience for the baby with good eye contact & positioning?		*Warmth – Appropriate clothes, bedding, attention and response to room & outdoor temperature?*
Hygiene – Change nappy regularly/when needed, wash hands after changing nappy, provide clean appropriate sized clothes, Wash/bathe daily and thoroughly?		*Understanding and responding to the baby's needs*

2. Emotional warmth

Is child held & handled with due care? Is child held facing towards or away from parent?		*Is baby cuddled frequently – do parent & baby enjoy this? Eye contact?*
How does parent respond to baby's distress? Can s/he show appropriate concern, respond to and tolerate the distress, calm/ soothe the baby? If older baby/toddler, can she distract appropriately?		*Does parent initiate play/contact with baby? Does s/he respond to baby's cues that s/he wants interaction?*
Is parent intrusive – overexcite baby – not able to pick up on the baby's cues when tired, scared, etc? Is s/he focused or too easily distracted from the baby (e.g. texts, phone calls, TV)?		

3. Parent's ability to stimulate

Does parent talk to the baby – how much/how often/tone of voice. Does s/he introduce toys / activities that are appropriate and stimulate vision, touch, and hearing?		*Is baby placed on the floor to play and to improve posture skills on back & tummy as well as time in a baby seat/ buggy & being held?*
Does s/he take the baby out for a reasonable length of time?		
Is parent intrusive – overexcite baby – not able to pick up on the baby's cues when tired, scared etc? Is s/he focused or too easily distracted from the baby (e.g. texts, phone calls, TV)?		

4. Ensuring safety

Is the sudden infant death prevention advice followed? (Sleep on back, bedroom not too hot/not too much bedding, no sleeping with parent, no smoking near baby/position in cot with feet to bottom of cot)		*Are adult friends/ partners safe? Parent's awareness of personal safety?*
Is s/he able to think ahead to be aware of hazards – i.e. hot drinks near baby, sharp objects, hot radiators, stairs, strapped in, etc?		*Capacity to accept guidance?*

5. Budget management, provision of food, nappies and clothing

Are the child's essentials the priority? Is spending in proportion to what is needed and how much money is available?	
Who is purchasing items? Who is thinking ahead about what is required? Are there debts to be paid off?	

6. Ability to respond to advice and support

Provide any examples.	

7. Parent's presentation in placement

Is parent engaged and motivated in parenting task?	

8. Time out of placement

How is this negotiated? Time keeping. Does time out impact on baby's routines?	

9. Maintenance of bedroom

Ability to provide clean, tidy and safe environment.	

10. Any other observations

11. Any other specific concerns

Foster carer signature

Date

Comments of Parent:

I confirm that I have read the above notes

Parent's signature

Date